HOPKINSTOWN 1911
A WELSH RAILWAY DISASTER

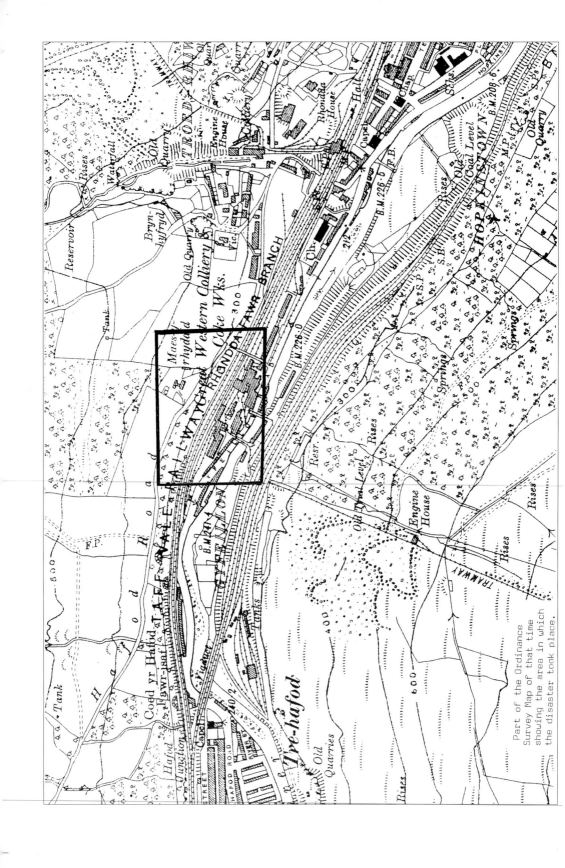

Part of the Ordinance Survey Map of that time showing the area in which the disaster took place.

HOPKINSTOWN 1911

A WELSH RAILWAY DISASTER

DAVID J. CARPENTER

TEMPUS

Frontispiece: Part of the Ordnance Survey map of that time, showing the area in which the disaster took place.

First published 2005

Tempus Publishing Limited
The Mill, Brimscombe Port,
Stroud, Gloucestershire, GL5 2QG
www.tempus-publishing.com

© David J. Carpenter 2005

British Library Cataloguing in Publication Data.
A catalogue record for this book is available from the British Library.

ISBN 0 7524 3250 8

Typesetting and origination by Tempus Publishing Limited.
Printed in Great Britain.

Contents

Acknowledgements

I would like to thank the following people for their help, suggestions, and guidance in the compilation of this book. Without their assistance the book would not have been published. I apologise to anyone whose name has been omitted from the following list: Mr Nick Kelland, Treorchy Library; Mr Howell Mathews, Pontypridd Library; Mr David Ellis, sexton, Trealaw Cemetery; Mr Keith Davies, sexton, Treorchy Cemetery; Mr Jeff Coombs, sexton, Ferndale Cemetery; Mr Terry Davies, Glyntaff Cemetery; Revd F. Melville K. Jones, vicar of St Illtud's Church, Llantwit Fadre; Ms Carolyn Charles and Mr Peter Bennet, Dept. of Industry, National Museum of Wales, Nantgarw; Mr and Mrs Bill and Yvonne Taylor, Llantwit Fadre, Mr Douglas Pearce, Caerphilly, and Mr E.M. Jenkins, Treherbert.

David J. Carpenter.

Introduction

In the early part of the twentieth century, the people of the mining valleys and the surrounding areas grew up in an environment which was, and had been for many years, fraught with danger and the proximity of death as a result of the numerous accidents and catastrophes in the various collieries, and the effect they had on close-knit families, local communities, and indeed on the valleys as a whole. Many stories have been written on these tragedies and the bravery and unselfishness of the people involved. They stand as a testimony to the hardships experienced in the valleys, as the majority of these disasters involved the deaths of men and boys working in the local collieries. However, despite all this, the train disaster which occurred one fateful day in January 1911 shocked not only the mining communities of both the Rhondda Fawr and Fach valleys but also a large area of the South Wales Coalfield. This disaster was different; it involved people of all ages, people who had been going about their normal routines and business without any thought of danger.

When news of the disaster and details of the dead and injured became known, a tremendous feeling of shock and disbelief spread throughout the villages of the Rhondda. Many of the dead were well-known in their localities and held in high esteem, and of course, many were children.

After spending two years intermittently researching this disaster, I have written this book on the tragedy and hope that the reader will be able to fully appreciate the hardships and sorrow experienced by the families and communities in those difficult times.

David J. Carpenter.

References

Publications

Railway and Industrial Heritage of Pontypridd and District
    1985 Taff Ely Council.
The Gateway to the Rhondda, David J. Rees, 1979.
Rails in the Valleys, James Page, 1989.
Taff Vale Railway Miscellany, John Hutton, 1988.
South Wales Branch Lines, H. Morgan. 1984.
A Tribute to the 'Servants of Steam' (150th Anniversary of the Taff Vale
    Railway), 1991.

Newspapers
Rhondda leader
Pontypridd Observer
Glamorgan Free Press
Glamorgan County Times.
The Weekly Mail
Cardiff Times
Cardiff & Merthyr Guardian
South Wales Echo
Western Mail

one

The Disaster
and its Victims

Monday 23 January 1911 started as a grey, damp morning, normal for this time of the year, with people reluctantly leaving their warm beds in order to catch the train to their places of work or business. The fateful train which left Treherbert at 9.10 a.m. precisely, whose engine was a 0-6-2 type U class No.193 and which was controlled by driver Allex Sellars, meandered down through the valley, stopping at each station to pick up passengers until it reached Porth Station at approximately 9.30 a.m. At this station the engine was uncoupled whilst two additional coaches, originating from Maerdy, were attached to the front of the Treherbert section, bringing the number of passengers travelling to about 200. The engine was recoupled 'chimney first', not 'bunker first'. (This later became common practice on the valley lines).

The streets at that time in the morning were unusually quiet, due to the National Strike which was taking place in the coalfield. There was not the usual hustle and bustle normally associated with the collieries, such as the whistle from the colliery hooters, the marching and the banter of conversation from the miners going to and from the colliery for their shifts, the clanging from the shunting of the coal wagons and the sound of the steam engine. But it was as normal a day as it could be in these circumstances, for now.

The train left Porth at 9.40 a.m. Among the passengers were many local dignitaries who were proceeding to Cardiff in order to continue their business, or perhaps catch the train to London or other parts of England. It would appear that this was the most popular and most convenient train used for that purpose, but on that particular day many of the local dignitaries and other public figures had pressing business within their own localities due to the National Strike and did not catch the train. All went well until the coke ovens, situated about a mile and a half from Pontypridd, were reached at around 9.48 a.m. The presence of mist that day and the curve of the line made visibility poor. As the train came around the bend near Crockets Place, Hopkinstown, a mineral train consisting of about thirty to forty trucks of coal was stationary along the same track as the passenger train. Whilst there was seemingly no chance of avoiding a collision, the driver very quickly applied the brakes in hopes of minimising the force of the crash. But within seconds there was a terrific impact, with the engine of the Treherbert train leaving the rails and shattering the brake van of the mineral train and damaging some of the mineral trucks.

Treherbert Station. It was from this station that the ill-fated train journey started, and unfortunately some of the passengers who boarded were victims of the impending tragedy.

The crash was followed by the frenzied screams of the passengers, many of whom were trapped in the first carriage at impact. Frantic efforts were made by the passengers to get out, but doors and windows were jammed shut. Many managed to clamber out through other doors or windows, and others were pulled to safety by people who had gathered outside.

By coincidence, at almost the same moment an up train which had been travelling at a fairly rapid rate pulled up dead opposite the scene of the accident. Many of the passengers from this train quickly give aid and offered what assistance they could by helping people from the wrecked coaches.

The scene was one of utter devastation; piled on top of one another was a shapeless wreck of carriages, which were in many instances – due to the force of

Tonypandy was the most popular station on the line at that time, which resulted in a large number of passengers boarding the train here daily. Two who boarded here on the morning of 11 January 1911 later died in the crash.

A view showing the entrance to the station at the end of Station Street, Porth. Note the large number of people making their way to the station.

Railway Station,
Porth. 1000.

This is a view of the main railway station which serves both Rhondda valleys, the Fawr and the Fach. At Porth at that time it was normal procedure to affix extra coaches to the train, which had started out from Maerdy Station to the train from Treherbert Station, and then continued to Pontypridd and Cardiff.

Many of the crash victims caught the train at Maerdy Station, pictured here, to meet up with the Rhondda Fawr train at Porth and proceed from there to Pontypridd and Cardiff.

impact – reduced to matchwood. Columns of hissing steam were emitted by the derailed engine, whilst immediately in front was all that remained of the rear portion of the coal train. The guard's van, which had been reduced to pulp, was the scene of the greatest part of the disaster. The van, which was placed immediately behind the engine, was telescoped into the first seven compartments of the first coach and it was in these compartments that the largest number of fatalities occurred; other fatalities were mainly due to the destruction of the carriages.

Doctors and ambulance men were quickly on the scene and the dead and injured were removed to the nearby engine sheds, which were used as a first-aid station and makeshift mortuary. There the dead were reverently covered to await identification, whilst the injured were prepared to be conveyed by special train to Cardiff Infirmary for treatment.

After identification, the list of names of those who died read as follows:

Councillor Tom George, Ferndale. Miners' checkweigher.
Councillor H. Morgan, Treherbert. Financial secretary of No.1 Lodge, Rhondda. Miners' checkweigher at the Fernhill Colliery.
Councillor Tom Harries, Pontygwaith. Miners' checkweigher at No.8 pit, Tylorstown.
Miss Margaret Davies (aged ten), daughter of Mr Jack Davies, Commercial Hotel, Ferndale.
Mr Thomas John Hodges, butcher, High Street, Ferndale.
Master Thomas Ivor Hodges (aged nine), his son.
Revd Landeck Powell, Calvinistic Methodist Minister, Caerphilly.
Miss Hannah Jenkins (aged sixteen), Morgan Street, Trehafod. Daughter of Mr Edward Jenkins, collier, Trehafod.
Mr Edward Lewis, horse dealer, Pontrhondda Farm, Llwynypia.
Mr Idris I.M. Evans (aged eighteen), articled clerk, Llwynderw, Tonypandy.
Mr Lodwig Hughes (aged thirty-seven), colliery engine driver, of James Street, Mardy.

Those injured were taken with all speed by a special ambulance train to Cardiff Infirmary for further treatment to their injuries.

They were: Mr Wyndham Morris, clerk, 16 Ebenezer Terrace, Newport, who suffered terrible fractures of both legs and in consequence of these injuries had to have one of his legs amputated at the Infirmary. (Due to the lack of information, the degree of amputation could not be established.)

Mr George Gould, guard of the coal train, 15 Treherbert Street, Cathays Cardiff, who had cuts to the face, head and arms, and was suffering from shock.
Mr Rowland Wolby, collier, 11 Kennard Street, Ton-Pentre, who had cuts on his face and was suffering from shock.

Mrs Annie Bonnett, 47 Brynwyndham Street, Treherbert, who suffered cuts on her head and face, and was suffering from shock.

Mrs Hodges, (whose husband and son were killed in the tragedy), High Street, Ferndale, who was badly cut about the head.

Mrs R. Davies of 58 Brynhowell Terrace, Ynyshir, was able to proceed home after her injuries (to the back of her head) were treated at the emergency first-aid station. She was accompanied by her husband, who had not been injured.

Note:

Mr Wolby and Mrs Bonnett were allowed home after treatment. Mrs Hodges and Mr Morris remained at the hospital for further treatment, which was to prove successful. Unfortunately, this was not the case with Mr George Gould. He had been admitted into the hospital with what was thought to be superficial cuts and shock. However, it was found that, besides the external cuts and bruises, he had a broken arm and suffered internal injuries. Despite receiving treatment for two months, he died on 25 March 1911, leaving a widow and three children.

This increased the number of unfortunate victims to twelve.

A selection of newspaper clippings illustrating the
immediate reactions to the disaster

From *Rhondda Leader*, Saturday 28 January 1911.

SATURDAY, JANUARY 28, 1911

No. 583

Train Disaster at Hopkinstown.

Terrible Collision between Passenger and Mineral Trains.

Eleven Passengers Killed.

Three Miners' Leaders Among the Victims.

Engine Derailed and Coaches Wrecked.

Touching Identification Scenes.

Story of the Disaster.

Some Marvellous Escapes.

I arrived on the scene, writes our Special Correspondent, just as the body of Councillor W. H. Morgan was being reverently borne to the engine sheds. What I saw almost baffles the ingenuity of man to describe. Piled on top of one another was the shapeless wreck of carriages, the greater portions of which had been reduced to matchwood by the terrible force of the impact. At the far end of this wreckage arose a white column of hissing steam, emitted by the derailed engine, while immediately in front was all that remained of the rear portion of the heavy coal train which had worked the mischief. The guard's van was literally reduced to pulp, whilst several trucks containing Lewis Merthyr coal were thrown in all manner of ways across the permanent way as if Jove had hurled them from the neighbouring crag of Pontygraigwen.

From *Rhondda Leader*, Saturday 28 January 1911.

The scene at the engine shed was pathetic in the extreme. The bodies were placed in a row, and had to be repeatedly uncovered in order to facilitate the task of identification by friends and relatives who were speedily on the spot from all directions. The identity of the three miners' agents was established by a Pontypridd reporter, who counted them among his intimate friends. Little difficulty was experienced with the identification of the others, with the exception of the body of Lodwig Hughes, whose identity was eventually secured by his name being engraved on the watch in his waistcoat pocket.

17

Thrilling Narratives.

Survivors Tell of Hairbreadth Escapes.

Thrilling narratives have been given by survivors of the catastrophe. Mr. J. D. Williams, J.P., said that all of a sudden there was a severe bump, and he immediately knew that something was wrong. A portion of the next carriage had been knocked in by the guard's van, and four or five of its occupants were killed. What affected him most of all was the dead body of his colleague on the District Council, Mr. Tom George, Ferndale. He was standing as if he were looking out through the window, having been forced into that position by the pressure of the woodwork around him. "I have never seen anything like it before," added Mr. Williams, "and I hope I shall never experience anything like it again."

Mr. Wm. Phillips, registrar of marriages, said in a conversation with a Pressman that he had had a miraculous escape. He attributed his escape to immediately jumping to the carriage window when he heard the crash, and no sooner had he done so than timbers came crashing through the roof.

Above and opposite: From *Rhondda Leader*, Saturday 28 January 1911.

Metro's and Soldiers Guard Railway.

News of the accident spread like wild-fire throughout the surrounding districts, and ere a few minutes had elapsed the bank overlooking the railway was like a theatre gallery, every inch of foothold being occupied by thousands of spectators, who watched the rescuing operations with morbid curiosity. Detachments of the Metropolitan Police and the West Riding Regiment were also soon on the scene, and lent valuable assistance in keeping the crowds from encroaching upon the railway. The troops brought stretchers with them, and these were utilised for the conveyance of the dead into the engine-house and the removal of the injured into the train in which they were taken to Cardiff for treatment at the infirmary.

All day long the work of clearing the wreckage proceeded apace, large cranes being brought into service, which were so powerful that when chains had been fastened around the smashed carriages they were lifted bodily off the line. By the early evening the wreckage had been almost entirely removed.

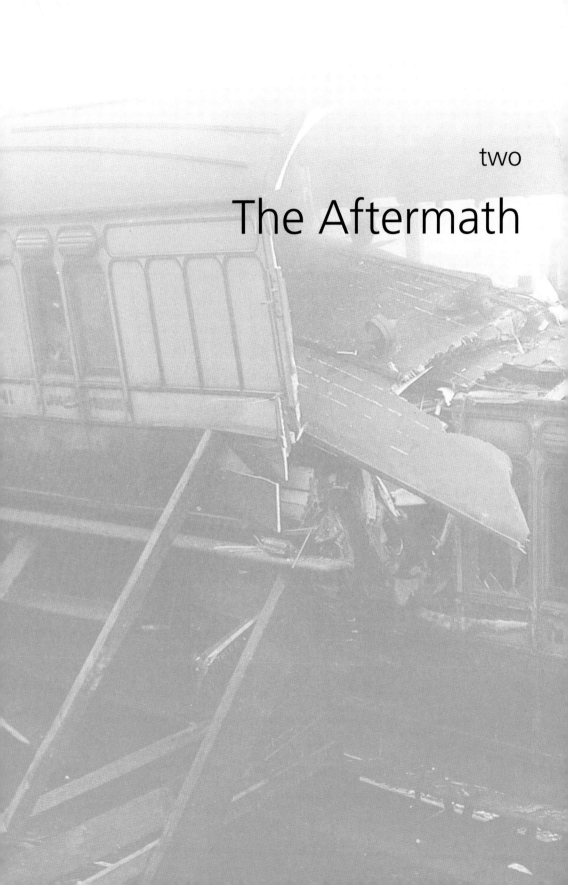

two

The Aftermath

News of the disaster spread throughout the surrounding areas and it was not long before a large number of people were standing around in morbid curiosity, watching the rescue operations. Detachments of the Metropolitan Police and the West Riding Regiment (already in the area due to the National Coal Strike) were quickly on the scene in order to control the rapidly enlarged crowd of spectators from encroaching on the line, and thus hampering rescue operations, and to help the rescue attempt by bringing with them essential first-aid equipment, such as stretchers in which to move the casualties to the emergency first-aid station and later to the special train to take the injured to Cardiff. All day long the work of clearing the wreckage continued, with large cranes being brought into service which enabled the smashed carriages to be bodily lifted from the line onto flat carts, which proceeded to remove them from the disaster area. By the early evening the wreckage had been almost entirely removed.

The chief constable, Captain Lionel Lindsay, together with Deputy Chief Constable Cole, and inspectors Salter and Williams, conferred with the district coroner, Mr R.J. Rhys, regarding the arrangements for the removal of the bodies of the deceased. A Coroners' Jury was duly summoned and, after viewing the bodies, gave permission for them to be removed. At the same time it was announced that the inquest on the tragedy would take place at Pontypridd Police Station on Thursday 26 January 1911, at 9.30 a.m.

The emotional strength of feeling in the makeshift morgue was unbelievable. The bodies had been placed in a row in order to make it easier for relatives and friends to identify their loved ones, but it did not help matters that they had to be repeatedly uncovered in order to facilitate the task of identification. The identification of the three miner's agents was carried out by a reporter who was a personal friend of each of them. Little difficulty was experienced with the identification of the others, with the exception of Mr Lodwig Hughes, whose identity was finally established by his watch, in which his name had been engraved.

The scenes in which the child Margaret Davies, aged ten, was identified by her father, Mr Jack Davies, landlord of the Commercial Hotel, Ferndale, were touching in the extreme. In the case of poor Mrs Hodges, Ferndale, all those present were greatly distressed, as she had to identify the bodies of her husband Thomas and her nine-year-old son, also named Thomas, despite being badly injured herself.

Mrs Hodges stated that, as she slowly recovered from the crash, she could see her husband was dead, and that her son Thomas was injured just like herself. She held him to her for comfort, but he died in her arms. Such was the highly charged

General view showing the scene of the disaster.

atmosphere that when she left to go to Cardiff for treatment there was not a dry eye left in the building.

After the identification of the victims had formally taken place they were conveyed to their homes, some by road, others by rail, and were met at their destinations by crowds of sympathetic people.

The injured who had been sent to Cardiff were promptly examined when they arrived at the infirmary and George Gould, Rowland Wolby and Mrs Annie Bonnett were treated for shock, and cuts to the arms and face, but were allowed to return home after treatment. Mrs Hodges was found to be badly cut around the head and remained at the hospital for treatment together with Mr Wyndham Morris, who was found to have two fractured legs, with the right leg being so badly damaged that it became necessary to amputate.

Miraculous Escapes

Many miraculous escapes were recounted in connection with the disaster from those who survived.

The driver of the passenger train (Alec Sellars) his stoker (John Jones) were at the point of impact but somehow escaped without any form of injury. However, they were in a dazed condition and confused by what was occurring around them.

The guard of the rear van of the coal train, George Gould, was again at the point of impact but escaped with severe cuts and bruises.

The guard of the front passenger van (Mr T. Godwin) stated that when the van smashed into the second passenger coach, the flooring of the van burst upwards forcing him almost to the roof of the van, but without causing him any injury. After the vehicles had settled after the impact he managed to clamber out of the van and, although suffering from shock, was able to render assistance to the rescuers.

Mr William Phillips, registrar of marriages, attributed his miraculous escape from injury to the fact that immediately he heard and felt the crash he rushed to the window in order to ascertain what was happening; at just that point, timbers came crashing through the roof and landed exactly where he had been sitting just moments before.

Councillor William Jenkins, Cymmer, Port Talbot, said that he usually changed carriages when he got to Porth so as to join his Rhondda Fach colleagues, but on this occasion he remained in his compartment with Mr Walters, a Treherbert

View showing telescoped carriage in which the victims died.

The search for victims of the crash.

grocer. Had he followed his usual habits, he would have undoubtedly either been killed or seriously injured.

A young Porth collier attributed his escape to a young lady that he knew. He was looking out of his carriage window when he saw the young lady having difficulty in opening her carriage door. He got out to assist her, and then decided to travel in the same carriage with her. Had he returned to his first carriage he would have been killed, as he had been sitting with the three unfortunate Miners' agents.

Mr Benjamin Cole, a builder of Ton-Pentre, seemed to have had a premonition of disaster. He declined to accompany a friend to the front carriages of the train, but persuaded his friend to enter a compartment in the middle of the train; no one in their coach was injured.

Mr Tom Williams, an official of Pontypridd District Council, also had a narrow escape. He normally sat at the front of the train with his two very good friends, councillors Tom George and Tom Harries. For some reason which he could not explain, he did not do so that day, but went instead to a rear compartment.

Two other people who should have been on that train possibly owe their lives to circumstance. William Abraham (Mabon) had intended to have been on the train with the councillors who were killed and probably would have suffered the same fate. However, Federation business in connection with a conference on Tuesday

A general view of the collision.

A view showing the telescoped coaches.

compelled him to travel to London on the preceding Sunday. The other, Miss Greta Morris, daughter of Morris Builders, Ferndale, missed the train due to her watch happily being seven minutes late.

One of the strangest stories that occurred was that of Police Inspector Hole's daughter. Miss Hole attended school at Pontypridd, and usually travelled on the train from Tonypandy. She was a passenger on the wrecked train and after the crash stepped from her compartment, which had not been damaged, to walk to the road. Here she caught the tram to Pontypridd and visited the police station and calmly told the police of the accident, and telephoned her parents to inform them that she was safe. Quite calm and collected, she then continued to school and joined her class as though the disaster had not occurred. She was just thirteen years old!

Another extraordinary escape was experienced by Mr Mordecai Thomas, of Ferndale. He had intended to travel on that particular train on Monday morning and he was planning to take his dog with him. At the booking office he obtained a ticket for himself and his dog. He then realised that the dog had slipped its lead and had run from the station. He hurried off in pursuit and after catching the animal returned to the station, only to see the train departing from the station.

The guard of the passenger train, Mr John White, had to vacate the front guard's van at Trehafod due to the amount of freight loaded into it and continued his journey by travelling on the central guard's van. As the front guard's van was shortly reduced to pulp due to the impact, this situation probably saved his life.

Below and overleaf: From *Pontypridd Observer*, 28 January 1911.

PONTYPRIDD OBSERVER

TERRIBLE RAILWAY CALAMITY.

11 KILLED; 5 BADLY INJURED.

THREE LABOUR LEADERS KILLED.

SOME AGONISING SCENES.

Pontypridd and District was startled early on Monday morning by a rumour which gained credence that a collision had occurred on the Taff Vale Railway in the vicinity of Pontypridd. Later advice proved that the rumour was only too well founded on fact and the mournful news was flashed to all parts of the country.

The scene of the accident was a spot near the Coke Ovens, Hopkinstown, which is a busy junction about half a mile from Pontypridd Station, where the Taff Vale Co. carry on shunting operations on a somewhat extensive scale. The 9 a.m. train ex. Treherbert had made its journey as usual without any eventful incident to Porth, where a couple of carriages from Ferndale were shunted on to the front part of the train. Aboard were many business people proceeding to Pontypridd, and a number of prominent miners' leaders who were on their way to the Labour conference. As the train wended its way at a good speed around the slight curve near Hopkinstown the driver suddenly noticed a mineral train standing a short distance in front. Immediately his hand went to the brake, but too late—a terrific car splitting crash, then a silence, followed by the harsh sound of splintering woodwork and the crashing of glass. It was all over in a few seconds and from the

TERRIBLE WRECK

of what had once been complete carriages arose mingled moans, cries and screams. Men engaged on the yard looked aghast, and too dazed to move. The spell was broken by some of the passengers from the rear portion of the train scrambling out on to the line and the onlookers assisted them in an endeavour to free the imprisoned ones. Mr. Oscar Hurford, the Pontypridd stationmaster, appeared on the scene almost immediately and with commendable promptitude and zeal he directed the attempts at rescue. The train presented an extraordinary sight. The engine had left the rails and its strong steel framework was bent and twisted like wire. The following guard's van had been hurled bodily on top of the second carriage, smashing in the roof and clearing away the first few compartments like a scythe, dealing

DEATH AND DESTRUCTION

Births and Marriages, Porth, who was travelling in the third compartment of the second coach. He was observed at the window shouting for help and as the door on that side was locked it had to be smashed before he could be rescued from his dangerous position. Mr. Phillips says his escape is due to the fact that when he heard the crash he jumped to the window for as soon as he had done so the guard's van ploughed its way

THROUGH THE ROOF.

It was from the same compartment that Miss Hannah Jenkins, of Trehafod, was taken. Mr. Phillips himself assisting in removing her although himself suffering from a hurt to the back and legs. That the young lady was fatally injured was a fact at once apparent, her head being badly cut and her face and clothes covered with blood. Two other men who were also in the same compartment were pinned underneath the wreckage.

About mid-day it was possible to realise the full extent of the terrible disaster. The victims were:—

KILLED.

Councillor Tom George, Ferndale, check-weigher.

Councillor W. H. Morgan, Treherbert, checkweigher at the Fernhill Colliery and financial secretary of the No. 1 Lodge Rhondda Miners.

Councillor Tom Harris (39), 89, Madeline Street, Trehafod, checkweigher at No. 8 Pit, Tylorstown.

Mr. Edward Lewis, horse dealer, Pont Rhondda Farm, Llwynypia.

Mr. Lodwig Hughes, colliery engine driver, Mardy.

Miss Margaret Davies (10), daughter of Mr. Jack Davies, Commercial Hotel, Ferndale.

Mr. Thomas Jno. Hodges, manager for Eastmans, Ltd., 42, High Street, Ferndale.

Master Thomas Ivor Hodges (9), son of the above.

Rev. W. L. Powell, Calvinistic Methodist minister, Twyn Church, Caerphilly.

Miss Hannah Jenkins (16), 43, Morgan Street, Trehafod, draper's assistant in the employ of Mr. Compton Evans Taff Street, Pontypridd, and daughter of Mr. Edward Jenkins, collier, Trehafod.

Mr. Idris J. M. Evans (18), Llwynderw, Tonypandy, articled clerk to Messrs. Jones, Pughe, and Davey, Pontypridd.

INJURED.

The following were badly injured and had to be taken to the Cardiff Infirmary for treatment :—

Mr. Whyndam Morris (27), clerk; living

the engine driver (Alec. Sellers) or fireman (Jack Jones) could see the train in front before they got to within very few yards of it owing to the and the confused view caused by number of waggons on the metals a spot. Both men acted pluckily in s ing on the footplate.

IDENTIFICATION OF THE DEA

A small group of police stood as g ians of the engine shed wherein re the bodies of the eleven victims wh met such an awful and tragic fate, people desirous of entry were subj to close and searching scrutiny. forces of the law and order realised well and quite rightly that here w place for morbid sightseers, whose aim was to satisfy their natural curi by gazing at the blood-stained fac the victims, distorted in their agony, and with cruel gaping wo where the wreckage had wrought it work. In one long row along the of the engine shed they lay rigid u cover of wraps, and the full extent o catastrophe could be gleaned by g at the row of

Silent & Motionless

forms, whose thread of life had snapped with but short notice, and truly than ever did one realise that the midst of life we are in death." casionally a small group would app the shed and securing admittance would, dry eyed and fearful, gaze at dea dface which was reverently covered by one of the officials. A shake of the head and slowly they w pass along scanning each face, per with a wild hope that after all their one was safe. Another face unco and a moment's gaze would be foll by an outburst of weeping and the rowing relative would be conveyed the shed. It was heart-rending and work calculated to test the hea the stoutest and even the stolid seemingly implacable policemen at times constrained to turn a The bodies of the three miners' le were identified by a local pressman not much difficulty was experience identifying the others. The last t identified was the body of Mr. Lo Hughes, of Mardy, and this identific was facilitated by the discovery o police of the name on his watch. Jack Davies's grief when he recog the lifeless form of his little dau was pitiable. She had left her hon order to return to her school at Port after a week-end visit. During afternoon Mr. R. J. Rhys (district oner) arrived on the scene and a h

MEDICAL ASSISTANCE

was immediately telephoned for and in an incredibly short space of time numer-ous doctors from Pontypridd and dis-trict were on the scene, as also was Mr. Davison and his ambulance squad from the Great Western Colliery, which is not very far away from the scene of the ac-dent, and surely the value of the modern training for first aid work was never more adequately exemplified. The work of rescue was attempted as expe-ditiously as possible and it was a pro-ceeding attendant by some considerable danger by virtue of the splintered con-dition of the coaches. One by one the dead and

INJURED WERE EXTRICATED

and tenderly borne away. Some of the injured expired almost immediately on being taken out and these were carried to the hastily improvised mortuary in the engine shed near at hand. A pa-thetic feature was the discovery of a Ferndale family, Mr. and Mrs. and master Ivor Hodges. Mr. Hodges was dead when found, and the lad expired in his mother's arms. She herself was very badly injured and her cries for "Ivor my poor Ivor," moved even the hardest man to tears. They were going to the Cardiff Infirmary where the lad was to have undergone treatment for his eye-sight. In another compartment in the wrecked front coach was discovered the bodies of the three members of the Rhondda Urban District Council, all of whom were prominent Labour leaders. The Rev. Landeg Powell, of Caerphilly, was travelling in the middle coach and was the only passenger killed in that part of the train. At first it was thought the number of dead would not exceed four or five, but unfortunately this was not so, and as the work proceeded

ELEVEN BODIES

were placed in the shed near by.

As time passed huge crowds of people flocked to the scene until the high bank on the side of the line was a veritable sea of faces, and the services of the Metropolitan Police and the West Riding regiment who are stationed in Ponty-ridd in connection with the Mid-Rhondda industrial dispute, were re-quisitioned to prevent the crowd from encroaching on the railway and thus impeding the already arduous work of the willing helpers.

The breakdown gang arrived from Penarth Junction in a short time and Mr. T. E. Harland, superintendent of the line and other officials of the com-pany were quickly on the scene.

One of the narrowest escapes recorded that of Mr. Wm. Phillips, Registrar of

Mrs. Annie Bonnett, 47, Bryn Wyndham Street, Ferndale. Shock and cuts on the head and face.

Mrs. Hodges, High Street, Ferndale. Badly cut about the head. (Hus-band and son killed.)

Two Ynyshir people, Mr. and Mrs. Davies, 58, Brynhowel Terrace, were also passengers in the badly wrecked second coach and though Mrs. Davies received an injury to the back of the head she was able to proceed home. Mr. Davies es-caped unhurt.

Nearly everyone in the train were of course badly shaken and several suffered from shock.

ADDITIONAL PARTICULARS.

The terrible force of the impact was plainly manifested by the manner in which the stout woodwork of the carriages had been smashed to matchwood. The guard of the mineral train had a miracu-lous escape from death, for his van was crushed like an egg-shell by the on-coming engine, and a couple of the trucks laden with coal were smashed up and the mineral scattered over the line. When the crash came Gould was forced almost to the top of the roof of his van and fortunately he was thrown headlong on to the bank alongside the railway, escaping with cuts and bruises and naturally suffering from shock. It was also a fortunate happening that the en-gine was affixed to the train the right way round, that is, with the burden towards the coaches, for had it been otherwise nothing could have prevented the driver and fireman from paying the penalty for their temerity in sticking to their posts by being crushed to death. Another providential escape was that of the front van guard of the passenger train. When the Ferndale portion of the train was shunted on at Porth he left his van and proceeded to the front van in order to check the parcels there. As there were not many he was enabled to return to his own van at Trehafod, and in the light of maturer events he is probably very thankful that he did for nothing but a merciful Providence could have saved him from a violent death had he remained in the front van. Another noteworthy feature of the accident was the escape of a number of rabbits, who were liberat-ed by the smash and who scampered all over the place. One of the bunnies was found alive and unhurt on the Tuesday imprisoned under the wreckage.

That the mineral train was quite in order in being on that particular section is an admitted fact but owing to the natural official reticence, the cause of the accident is shrouded in mystery for the present. It could not be expected that

TO CARDIFF INFIRMARY.

Soon after the accident a special am-bulance train arrived and after the in-jured had been rendered first aid by the doctors on the scene they were conveyed with all speed to the Cardiff Infirmary. Enquiries made to date result in the gratifying information that all are doing as well as could be expected.

CLEARING THE WRECKAGE.

Meanwhile the breakdown gang were busily employed in clearing the wreckage with the aid of some huge cranes. The work proceeded throughout the day and thousands of people congregated on the heights of Graigwen which overlook the scene of the collision to witness the con-cluding chapters of the tragedy. In keeping the spot tolerably clear General MacReady with his troops, Captain Lindsay (Chief Constable), D.C.C. Cole Inspector Salter, Inspector Williams (Porth) and strong detachments of the Glamorgan and Metropolitan Constabu-lary rendered invaluable service. Mr Oscar Hurford, the Pontypridd station-master, seemed indefatigable in his efforts. Mr. T. E. Harland (Superin-tendent of the line), Mr. Cameron (Loco Inspector), and Mr. W. H. Edwards, of the Engineering Department, were also early on the scene of the disaster.

SOME HAIR-BREATH ESCAPES.

It is a fortunate matter that the num-ber of passengers travelling on the train was not heavier than it was, though probably the nearest of the conflicting estimates is that there were about 100 aboard the train. Alderman W. H Mathias, J.P. (Porth), Councillor Thos. Griffiths, J.P. (Porth) and Councillor J. D. Williams, J.P. (Clydach Court), were travelling in the second and first compartments, which was the third coach on the train, and it is an amazing thing that no more damage was done than the cracking of a window in their coach. A railway official declared that this immunity from disaster might be attributed to the protective effect of the spring buffers with which the carriage was fitted. The three gentlemen were of course severely shaken but they de-scended to the line unhurt. When in-terviewed Mr J. D. Williams gave a graphic description of the scene. "The carriage in front was badly smashed," he said, "and screams arose from it. I saw a person who appeared as if he was looking out of the window and I was greatly affected by recognising the dead body of Tom George." He added that he had no doubt that he had been forced into the position by the wreckage. He also described how he had seen the little daughter of Mr. Jack Davies who, he said, had her face turned from the win-dow, but when she was taken out he saw

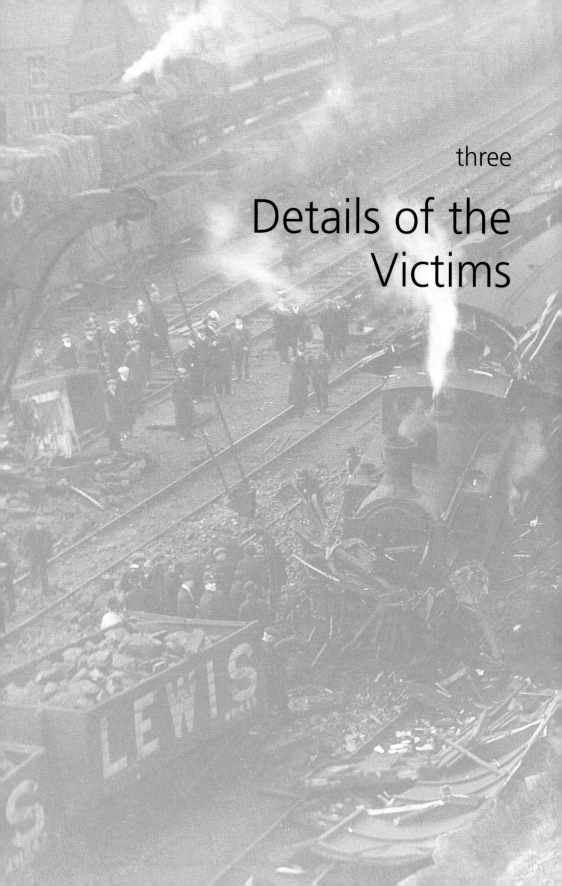

three

Details of the Victims

When news of the disaster spread throughout the district, the reaction was overwhelmingly one of shock and disbelief. When it was realised that children and young people were among the victims, untold sympathy was directed to the families of the victims. Messages of condolence abounded, and in the villages where the victims lived there was a feeling of despair and helplessness to comfort the families.

Repercussions from the disaster were also felt by the Rhondda miners, certainly in as much that three of the victims were prominent councillors, members of the executive committee of the South Wales Miners' Federation, and the representatives of the miners who were at that time involved in the National Miners' Strike across the whole of the South Wales Coalfield. Indeed, on that fateful morning they were proceeding to a special conference of the Miners' Federation of Great Britain in London, which had been convened to consider an application for financial support for 12,000 miners on strike at the Cambrian collieries in Mid-Rhondda. Their deaths would obviously cause problems, because not only were they involved in local negotiations but they were held in such high esteem by the miners they represented. One only has to realise the great efforts these men went to on behalf of their colleagues to appreciate the dread that quickly arose over forthcoming problems envisaged to be inevitable after their tragic deaths.

Brief Details of Some of the Victims

Tom George was born on 29 March 1852, in Aberdare. Lacking education in his younger days, he later attended evening classes in his spare time, with the result that he eventually succeeded in obtaining a First Class Manager's Certificate in Mining. He moved from Aberdare to Treorchy, where he worked for some time as a collier. He later moved to Ferndale, where he was employed at the local colliery as an official and played a prominent part in the strike of 1898. Soon afterwards he was appointed checkweigher at the colliery. He was around this time appointed on the executive council of the South Wales Miners' Federation, a position he held until the time of his death. In around 1902 he was elected a member of the Rhondda District Council, and at each election was always returned unopposed.

He was a keen Co-operator, and a prominent and active member of the Ferndale Industrial Co-operative Society Ltd, until his other commitments took him elsewhere. He was a deacon of Penuel (CM) Chapel, Ferndale, and, being a man of many talents, played the trombone in Caradog's famous choir, played the cello and was a successful choir conductor.

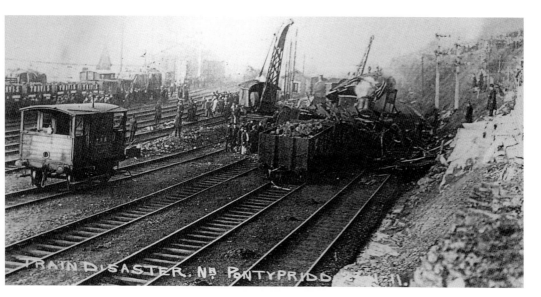

A view showing the cranes brought in to clear the wreckage.

Mr William Herbert Morgan as a young man attended schools at Treherbert where he received an elementary education. Like all youngsters of that time, he started work at the Fernhill Collieries. At the age of twenty-one he applied for the post of checkweigher at the collieries, and held that position until the time of his death. He furthered his education by attending evening classes and by home study. He then became a member of the executive council of the South Wales Miners' Federation and in 1908 became a member of the Rhondda Urban District Council for Ward No.1. On becoming a councillor, he founded the Treherbert Trades and Labour Council as he considered it his duty to keep the people of his constituency acquainted with his work on the council.

He was a man of refined habits and culture and spoke fluently in Welsh and English; he had also acquired a working knowledge of French and German. As a result of his fluency in mathematics he was elected to the position of financial secretary of the Rhondda District of the Miners' Federation. He excelled in financial affairs, and this proved to be of great service to the executive committee during important negotiations with the owners' side of the Coal Trade Conciliation Board. When the new Pontypridd and Rhondda Joint Water Board was established, he was appointed as one of the representatives on the new board. He was one of the mainstays of the Co-operative movement at Treherbert and a member of the central committee of the Ton Co-operative Society. He also held the posts of secretary of the Fernhill Workman's Institute, income tax commissioner for the County of Glamorgan, and compensation secretary for the Fernhill Lodge.

In the opinion of the people of Treherbert, whom he represented, 'WH', as he was popularly known, was regarded as a coming leader of the Welsh miners.

A view showing the crane lifting away the wreckage.

Mr Tom Harries was only thirty-nine years of age when he died. He was a religious man, totally devoted to his wife and family. As a leader of the miners, he was cool, deliberate, and of sound judgement. He did not rush into decisions; neither did he make rash statements. As a public servant and as a councillor, he was loyal, devoted and sincere. He always had the interests of the people he represented at heart and never sought to feather his own nest. His last public appearance was at the Pontygwaith Literary and Debating Society, when he gave an account of the work he had carried out throughout the year on their behalf.

After the death of these three prominent councillors, George, Morgan and Harries, who had during the Miners' strike been heavily involved in negotiations on behalf of the South Wales Miners' Federation, (SWMF) with the coal owners, it was necessary to appoint new negotiators to act on behalf of the federation.

To this end, Messrs Tom Smith, John Hopla, and Noah Rees, all members of the Cambrian Strike Committee, were appointed as members of the South Wales Miners' Federation, and began to continue the work which had been carried out by those men who had been killed in the train disaster.

Elizabeth Margaret Davies was the ten-year-old daughter of Mr and Mrs Jack Davies of the Commercial Hotel, Ferndale. Educationally, it would appear that she had a promising future ahead of her. She had spent twelve months at a boarding school at Cheltenham and at the time of her death was attending Mrs Brill's private school at Porthcawl.

Mr Thomas John Hodges, aged forty-three years, resided at Bristol Road, Maindee, Newport, and came to live in Ferndale when he was eighteen years old. He took up employment as an assistant at Messrs Eastmans, butchers. He was in later years promoted to manager, a position he held up to the time of his death. He married the daughter of Mr Tom Price, Lake Street, Ferndale. His son, Master Thomas Ivor Hodges who was just nine years old, died with him in the disaster.

Miss Hannah Jenkins, aged sixteen, resided at Morgan Street, Trehafod, Rhondda, where she lived with her father, Mr Edward Jenkins, and her mother. She was employed as an apprentice draper's assistant with Mr Compton Evans, Taff Street, Pontypridd. She usually travelled to Pontypridd on an earlier train, but she had a headache that morning and took the later train, and in so doing lost her life.

Mr Edward Lewis, aged thirteen, was a native of Llanidloes, but had lived the last eighteen years at Pontrhondda, Llwynypia. For many years he had a business as a haulage contractor, carrying out engagements for Rhondda Urban District Council, and the Cambrian Colliery Company of Clydach Vale. In later years he had traded as a horse dealer which required a large amount of travelling.

Mr Idris Isaac Morgan Edwards, aged eighteen, of Llwynderw, Tonypandy, was the son of the late Mr David Evans, draper, Excelsior Buildings, Tonypandy, and Mrs Elizabeth Naunton Evans. After receiving an elementary education at Tonypandy and Porthcawl, he attended Porth County School and then Porth Higher Grade School. He was then articled to Messrs Pughe-Jones and Davey, solicitors, Pontypridd, and was proceeding there on the morning of the disaster.

Mr Lodwig Hughes was brought up in Maerdy and started his working life at Mardy Colliery as a young man. He became a colliery engine driver and continued in this employment up to the time of his death. It would appear that he was held in the highest esteem, not only by those with whom he worked, but also by officials and management.

Revd W. Landeck Powell had held the Pastorate of Twyn Welsh CM Church, Caerphilly, for upwards of seven years and was greatly respected. He was returning from Tonypandy on the ill-fated train after fulfilling a preaching engagement at Pisgah CM Chapel at Penygraig on Sunday. He had stayed with his sister and brother-in-law (County Councillor James Evans) at Cambrian House, Clydach Vale, until the Monday morning. He was sixty years old when he met his death, and was born at Cwmamman in Carmarthenshire in 1850. He commenced preaching at Bethania, Aberdare, in 1874, and was educated at Trefecca College from 1875 to 1879. He was ordained to the Calvanistic Methodist Ministry at the Association Meeting at Aberystwyth in 1880. His first Pastorate was in charge of

A crane lifting the telescoped carriage from the wrecked train.

churches at Bettws and Ammanford in Carmarthenshire from 1879 to 1889. He then undertook an English Pastorate at Ogmore in Glamorganshire where he stayed until 1892 when he took over the Pastorate of Duffryn, Mountain Ash. Due to the delicate state of his wife's health he relinquished this position in 1894.

In 1903, on the departure of Revd W. Jones to America from the Twyn Chapel, Caerphilly, he became the pastor of this chapel, and by his gentle and kind disposition had become endeared, not only to those under his pastoral charge, but also to all who had come into contact with him.

Mr George Gould, aged fifty-five, was a native of Cardiff, and had been employed by the Taff Vale Co. for thirty-five years, and had been a guard for a considerable time. He was an active member of the company's ambulance brigade, and was also a well-known figure in Friendly Society circles, being connected with the Foresters. He was injured in the train disaster and, due to his injuries, died at Cardiff Infirmary two months after the tragedy. He left a widow and four children.

four

The Funerals of
the Victims

The victims of the train disaster were laid to rest at various cemeteries through-out the area between Thursday 26 to Saturday 28 January 1911, amid sympathetic scenes of mourning that affected virtually everyone living in the area. The funerals of the three councillors were impressive, with shops in their relative districts being shut, blinds drawn in private houses, and crowds lining the streets through which the funeral processions would proceed in order to pay their last respects.

Similar scenes, but ostentatious to a lesser degree, took place for the other victims, and deep sympathy was expressed by family groups, friends and associates who came together to pay their last respects to loved ones.

Such scenes throughout these trying days would remain in the memories of those people present for many years to come.

Details of the funeral arrangements for the unfortunate victims are as follows:

Thomas John Hodges, Thomas Ivor Hodges

The remains of Thomas John Hodges, and his son Thomas Ivor, were laid to rest at Ferndale Cemetery on Thursday afternoon on 26 January 1911. There was a large attendance of friends and relatives who had come to pay their respects to the deceased.

The officiating minister was Revd S.R. Wilkins, pastor of the English Westleyan Church, Ferndale, who paid glowing tributes to the deceased. When the cortege was about to enter through the gates of the cemetery, approximately sixty small boys, fellow students at the Ferndale Boy's School, stood at the gates and bowed their heads with reverence as a token of respect to the victims.

The chief mourners were: Mr and Mrs Jonathan Hodges, Newport, mother and father of Mr Hodges; (Mrs Hodges through her injuries was not able to attend); Mr and Mrs Tom Price, Ferndale (father and mother-in-law); Mr and Mrs Hodges, Taunton (brother and sister-in-law); Mr and Mrs Ben Hodges, Newport (brother and sister-in-law); Mr and Mrs J.G. Reakes, Newport (brother-in-law and sister); Messrs W. and D. Purnell, Newport (cousins); Mr W. Davies, Builth Wells (uncle); Mr and Mrs Roach, Merthyr (cousins); Messrs Jim, Will, and Clara Price, Ferndale (brothers- and sister-in-law); Mrs Jones, Coedpenmaen (aunt).

The coffins, which were of plain oak, were mounted with heavy brass fittings and conveyed to the cemetery in separate hearses, where they were covered with many floral tributes sent by relatives, friends, and employees; for example, from

Overgrown grave of Thomas John Hodges and his son, Thomas Ivor, buried at Ferndale Cemetery on 26 January 1911. (Ref. T69.con)

Merrs Eastmans Ltd, of Merthyr, Dowlais, Aberdare, and the Rhondda District; Ferndale Rifle Club (of which Mr Hodges was the treasurer); Ferndale Conservative Club; Ferndale Band and Musical Institute; Ferndale, Mardy, and Tylorstown butchers; and the deceased boy's Sunday school class and teacher, and his schoolmates and teachers at the boy's school. Messrs J. Lawson, South Wales manager, and J.A. Martin, district manager of Eastmans Ltd, also sent tributes, and many other floral tributes from different organisations came flooding in.

Revd William Landeck Powell

Caerphilly was in mourning on Thursday 26 January 1911, when the funeral of Revd William Landeck Powell, the CM Minister of Twyn Chapel, Caerphilly, took place. When the lengthy funeral cortege passed down the main street after leaving the family home Dolwen, every curtain in every shop and private home was drawn and all the local hotels were closed as a mark of respect to the deceased.

Among those present at the funeral were Sir Alfred Thomas, Revd C. Tawelfryn Thomas, Revd Connop L. Price (Rector of Caerphilly), the Revds J.O. Evans,

Family grave of Revd W. Landeck Powell, buried at St Martin's Church on 26 January 1911. (Ref. unknown)

Zoar, Bonvilstone; E.P. Jones, Cardiff; W.J. Williams, Hirwain; J.M. Davies, Aberfan; JP Jones, Cardiff; D.J. Evans, Merthyr; John Morgan, Aberdare; Evan Thomas, Sengenydd; and D.J. Howells and Ioan Thomas, Llanbradach; Dr T.W. Thomas; Messrs W. Davies, J.A. Phillips, D.T. Salathiel and others. Walking by the sides of the hearse bearing the magnificent oak coffin, furnished with heavy brass fittings and a suitably scribed breast plate, were the deacons of the chapel, Messrs E.T. Griffiths, E. Griffiths, E. Morgan and John John.

Immediately behind were the mourners; among them were Mr Powell (brother of the deceased), and his three brothers-in-law, Mr Griffiths, Mr Evans and Dr Morgan, all of Clydach Vale.

On arriving at Twyn Chapel an impressive service was held. Revd T.E. Davies conducted the service, assisted by Revd William Lewis, Cwmparc. Revd H.M. Ellis, Trealaw, delivered a touching sermon. All the ministers spoke of the good

Headstone details for
William Landeck Powell.

qualities of the deceased, and during the service Mr E.T. Griffiths read a telegram from Mr C. Edwards, MP for Caerphilly. The service ended with a rendering of the 'Dead March in Saul' by the organist.

The cortege then made its way to St Martin's churchyard where the interment took place. A large crowd awaited its arrival, and a very impressive ceremony took place. Assisting the officiating ministers was Revd Powell, Aberdare; Mr Griffiths and Connop L. Price, who had expressed a desire to assist, to show respect to a fellow Christian minister. Prayers were offered at the graveside by Revd W.J. Williams, Hirwain. The service concluded with the singing of a Welsh hymn.

Floral tributes were sent by the following:
'From Mary' (the widow); Twyn Chapel; Windsor Road Presbyterian Church, Caerphilly; Mr & Mrs E.T. Griffiths, Caerphilly; Mr & Mrs Charles, Chapel

House; Mr & Mrs W. Spickett, Caerphilly; and from his sisters at Pencae-Mawr.

Miss Elizabeth M. Davies.
The funeral of Miss Elizabeth Margaret Davies, the ten-year-old daughter of Mr and Mrs John Davies, Commercial Hotel, Ferndale, took place on Friday 27 January 1911 in the afternoon, with the remains being transported by road to Glyntaff Cemetery, Pontypridd.

The coffin, which was of polished oak, fitted with heavy brass handles and a plaque, was carried by a hearse and was totally covered with thirty-one floral wreathes sent by relatives and friends, and included tributes from: 'Papa, Mamma, and family'; 'Kathleen' (the maid), Principals and friends of Stanley College, Porthcawl; Mr and Mrs Pearson, Penywern College, Cheltenham; Governess and school friends of Penywern College, Cheltenham; Mr and Mrs Morgan Crowther, Cardiff; Mr and Mrs J.E. Sprague, Pontypridd; Dr T. Parry JP, Ferndale; Mr and Mrs F. Scott, Ferndale; Mr and Mrs Joe Ball, Pontypridd; Mrs E. Davies, Salisbury Hotel, Ferndale; Mr Tom Lloyd, Llanelly; Mr and Mrs A.E. Franks, manager, Ferndale Gas Company; and finally Pontypridd United Breweries Ltd, to name a few among the many.

Family grave of Elizabeth Margaret Davies, buried at Glyndaff Cemetery on 27 January 1911. (Ref. J24)

Headstone details of Elizabeth Margaret Davies.

The mourners who accompanied the cortege to the cemetery were:
Mr John Davies (father); Mr Jack Davies (brother); Mr Robert Davies, Pontygwaith (uncle); Mr J.E. Price, Mardy Hotel, Merthyr (uncle); Mr D. Rees, Merthyr, (uncle); Mr Israel Price, Merthyr (uncle); Mr J.E. Price, The Antelope, Dowlais, (uncle); and Mr Evan Jones, Merthyr (uncle).

The burial service was conducted by Revd B. Jones-Evans MA (vicar of Ferndale), assisted by Revd T. Davies (curate). Messrs T.E. Sealey, tobacconist, Ferndale; E.A. Franks, gas works, Ferndale; J.E. Sprague, Pontypridd; and W.D. Rees MRCVS, veterinary surgeon, acted as bearers.

Councillor Tom Harries

On Friday 27 January 1911, the mortal remains of Councillor Tom Harries were interred at Llethrddu Cemetery, Trealaw. Prior to this, a service was held at the family home in which Revd T.H. Jones, curate of St Mary Magdalene, read a portion of scripture, and Revd Joseph Evans, Soar, offered up prayer in Welsh.

The funeral was one of the largest experienced in Pontygwaith for many years, with large crowds paying their respects to the victim. The cortege was so long that it took approximately one hour to pass through the cemetery gates at Trealaw. The

Above left: Grave of Councillor Tom Harries buried at Llethrddu Cemetery, Trealaw, on 27 January 1911. (Ref. 01)

Above right: Headstone details of Councillor Tom Harries.

funeral arrangements were carried out by Messrs S. Rees and Co. and Revd T. Evans, Bethany, officiated and had charge of the burial service.

Floral tributes were from Mrs Harries (widow); Mrs Davies and family; Mr and Mrs Hughes, Grove House; Mr and Mrs D. Watts Morgan; Mr and Mrs D. Smith; Right Hon. W. Abraham, MP; the Conciliation Board; Rhondda Miners' Federation; Mrs W.P. Nichols; chairman and members of the Rhondda District Council; chief officials of the Rhondda District Council; clerical staff of the Rhondda District Council; headteachers and staff of schools; Rhondda NUT (National Union of Teachers); members of the Citizens' League; Bethany Congo Church; workmen of Nos 8 and 9 Pits, Tylorstown; Llwynypia Steam Coal Colliery workmen.

The chief mourners were: Mrs Harries (widow); Misses Tegwen and Annie and Master Tom J. Harries (children of the deceased); Misses Margaret, Blodwen, and Gertrude Davies (sisters-in-law); Mr Jack Davies (brother-in-law); Mr and Mrs W.

Davies, Cefn Coed; Mr and Mrs J. Williams; Mr W. Davies, Llandaff; Mr and Mrs D. Williams, Aberdare; Mrs King, Cefn Coed; Mr and Mrs Davies, Brynaman. The South Wales Miners' Federation was represented by Messrs T. Richards MP; W. Brace MP; Alfred Onions JP; Herbert Jenkins, W. Vyce, D. Morgan, and T. Lucas. Rhondda District of Miners was represented by Messrs D. Watts Morgan, L.R. Thomas and John Jones. The Labour and Liberal Association was represented by Messrs John Kemp and Morris Morris. Others present were: Messrs Edgar Jones MP; J. Rowland representing the Chancellor of the Exchequer; H.J. Abraham representing the Right Hon. W. Abraham MP; Mr J.D. Williams, Clydach Court; Messrs W. Morgan, Evan Williams, Fairfield; W.P. Nicholas; T.W. Berry; Dr. Chalke; Messrs Ben Davies JP, chairman of the Rhondda District Council, Octavius Thomasi; Revds Canon Lewis, D.J. Evans, D.M. Phillips and R.E. Salmon, Porth. Letters of sympathy were also received from many public bodies throughout the country, as well as from churches and public men.

At the graveside a portion of scripture was read by the vicar, Revd J. Rees. Afterwards, Mr T. Richards MP spoke of the great loss sustained by the death of Councillor Harries. He was a close personal friend of his, and was one of the most brilliant, thoughtful and cautious of the younger members of the executive. There was always a sweet reasonableness about him which won everybody's affection. The Rhondda miners, considering the special circumstances of the time, could ill afford to lose these three strong men, and he hoped worthy successors would be forth-coming.

Revd Rowland Hughes, BD, of Tylorstown, offered up prayers in Welsh, and Revd W. Williams gave out the hymn, 'Bydd myrdd O rfaddodau', which was sung as only Welshmen can sing it.

Mr Lodwig Hughes

On Friday 27 January 1911, the body of the late Mr Lodwig Hughes, of James Street, Mardy, one of the victims of the train disaster at Hopkinstown, was interred at St IItud's churchyard at Llantwit Fadre. The cortege proceeded by road to Llantwit Fadre, and joined the funeral of Miss Elizabeth M. Davies which was proceeding at that time to Glyntaff. A large number of friends of the deceased and his family left Mardy by train in order to meet the cortege at its destination.

The mourners were: Mrs Elizabeth Jane Hughes (wife); Mr Lewis (father); Ms Jenkins (sister); Mr Abednego Davies, manager of the Pentre (Cory) Collieries (brother-in-law); and many others.

Among those who went by train were Mr T.E. Richards, Mr H.E. Maltby (agent and manager of the Mardy Collieries) and Dr S. Glanville Morris. Others were the agent and sub-agent of the Winding Enginemen's Association, who together with a large crowd of friends had assembled at the house to pay their respects to a gentleman who was well-liked and respected by all who knew him.

Family grave of Lodwig Hughes buried at
St Iltud's churchyard on 27 January 1911.
(Ref. B45)

ER SERCHUS GOF AM
FY ANWYL BRIOD
LODWIG HUGHES,
JAMES ST. MAERDY,
YR HWN GOLLODD EI FYWYD
YN Y DDAMWAIN GYMERODD
LE AR REILFFORDD Y
TAFF VALE ION 23 AIN 1911
YN 37 MLWYDD OED.
AM HYNNY BYDDWCH
CHWITHAU BAROD CANYS YN
YR AWR NI THYBIOCH, Y DAW
MAB Y DYN.
ACHEFYD AM
ELIZABETH JANE HUGHES
BU FARW MEH 4-1952
YN 75 MLWYDD OED.
GWYN EU BYD Y RHAI PUR
O GALON.

Headstone details of Lodwig Hughes.

The directors of Locket's Merthyr Collieries, through their managing director, Mr W.H. Mewton, Llandaff, had instructed Mr T.E. Richards to convey their deepest condolences to the widow and father at the sad death of one who had as a boy commenced working at their collieries and had continued in their service throughout his life.

Revd J. Hope Evans and Revd D. Morris (All Saints' Church) conducted the service at the house and at the graveside.

Eight of the deceased's fellow enginemen acted as bearers.

Miss Hannah Jenkins

The funeral of Miss Hannah Jenkins, aged sixteen, the daughter of Mr and Mrs Edward Jenkins, Morgan Street, Trehafod, took place on Friday 27 January 1911. The service, which took place at Siloam CM Chapel, Trehafod, where the deceased was a member, was shared with another member of the chapel, Mrs Jones, Trehafod, who was also being buried that day, and was conducted by Revd T.P. Thomas.

After the service the cortege made its way to Glyntaff Cemetery, where the internment took place amidst a large crowd of family, friends, and neighbours.

Unmarked grave of Miss Hannah Jenkins, buried at Glyntaff Cemetery on 27 January 1911. (Ref. C877)

Extract from the *Pontypridd Observer*:

Date: Saturday, 28 January 1911.
Miss Hannah Jenkins's funeral took place on Friday 27 January 1911, and was rendered a joint one with another member of Siloam C.M. Chapel Trehafod, Mrs Jones, Trehafod, and Revd T.P. Thomas conducted a short service at that edifice. The funeral was very largely attended, the internment being at Glyntaff.
Note: Hannah Jenkins lived at Morgan Street, Trehafod. She was sixteen years of age when she died.
(Ref. C877.)

Mr Edward Lewis

The funeral of Mr Edward Lewis, Pontrhondda, Llwynypia, took place on Friday afternoon on 27 January 1911, with the deceased being interred at Llethrddu Cemetery, Trealaw. Mr Edwards had only been married just over two months and much sympathy was felt for his widow in her bereavement.

Mr Timothy Williams (Salem) officiated at the service in the house prior to the remains of the deceased being transported to the cemetery.

The mourners were: Mrs Lewis (widow); Mrs John Lewis, Pontygwaith (sister-in-law); Mrs Thomas Davies, Efail Isaf (cousin); Mrs and Miss Gardiner, Pontypridd; Mrs Tom Lewis, Llandiloes (sister-in-law); Mrs Holroyd Bradford (sister-in-law); Misses H. and M. Williams; Mrs David Lewis, Pontygwaith (sister-in-law); Mrs J. Haddrell, Treherbert (friend); Mr Francis Lewis (brother); Mr William Lewis, Merthyr (brother); Mr John Jarman, Llanidloes (step-brother); Mr Tom Hodgson, Bradford; Mr George Evans; Mr John Owen; Messrs Jarvis and Griffiths, Pentre; and Mr Richard Price, Tyntyla Road, Ystrad.

The service at the graveside was conducted by Revd D.T.R. James, vicar of Llwynypia, assisted by Revd A.G.A. Picton, curate of St Cynon's. The funeral arrangements were carried out by Messrs Williams and Sons, undertakers, Tonypandy.

Mr Idris I.M. Evans

The funeral of the late Mr Idris Isaac Morgan Evans of Llwynderw, Tonypandy, took place on Friday 27 January 1911. It was well attended, not only by a large number of local dignitaries, but a large number of the deceased's old school friends and work colleagues.

After an impressive service at the house, which was conducted by Revd M.H. Ellis (Trealaw), the cortege left for Llethrddu Cemetery, Trealaw. Included among the mourners were: Messrs L. Jillie and D. Trevor Evans (brothers); John

Right: Unmarked grave of Edward Lewis buried at Llethrddu Cemetery, Trealaw, on 27 January 1911. (Ref. B29)

Below: Collapsed headstone at the grave of of Idris Isaac Morgan Evans, buried at Llethrddu Cemetery Trealaw on 27 January 1911. (Ref. E.92)

Evans, Ynyshir; Dr Naunton Morgan, Gilfach Goch; Mr T. Naunton Morgan, Penygraig; Dr Idris N. Morgan, Tonypandy, and Revd T. Tissington, Cwmparc (uncles); Messrs Robert N. Morgan, Gilfach Goch; William Evans, Ynyshir; Reginald Jenkins, Merthyr Vale; Naunton Lewis, Cardiff; Ivor Evans, Penygraig (cousins); Messrs T.V. Jenkins, Merhyr Vale; Edward Lewis, Cardiff; John Evans, Penygraig; James Davies, Tonypandy; Evan Davies, Ynysybwl; David Davies, Ynysybwl; John Davies, Porth; T. Jones, Tonypandy; and Rees Phillips, Trehafod (uncles); and William and Eddie Evans, Ferndale (cousins). Others present were the Revds W. Williams, E. Walter Thomas, and Ambrose Williams; Alderman Richard Lewis, JP; Councillor D.W. Davies, JP; Councillor James Evans; Dr Ivor Davies; Messrs S. Owen Edwards; D.W. James; D.M. Williams; W.O. Jones; Llewelyn Evans; J. Kinstley; Willie Llewellyn; J. Cox; G. Barkway; G.W. Griffiths; Dan Charles; T.P. John; David Watkins; D.J. Jones; J. Owen Jones; J.W. Richards; Page Thomas; W.T. David; T. Evans, Tonypandy, and T. Jones (schoolmaster) Treherbert.

A magnificent number of wreaths adorned the hearse, many from the following: mother, brothers and sisters, grandmother and aunties, Revd and Mrs T. Tissington, Cwmparc (uncle and aunt); Dr Naunton and Mrs Ada Morgan, Gilfach Goch (uncle and aunt); Mr Edward and Rosa Lewis, Cardiff (uncle and aunt); Mr T.V. and Mrs Polly Jenkins, Merthyr (uncle and aunt); Dr Idris and Mrs Morgan, Tonypandy (uncle and aunt); Mr and Mrs Tom Naunton Morgan, Penygraig (uncle and aunt); Messrs Jones-Pughe and Davey, solicitors, Pontypridd; staff at Messrs Jones-Pughe and Davey, Pontypridd; teachers and pupils of Porth Higher Grade School; Messrs Griffiths and Pughe (Boots, cash chemists); Bob Cox, Exeter College; Maggie and Ivor Morgan, Penygraig (cousins); Mrs M.A. Evans, Aberdulais, near Neath; Mr Ed Jenkins, Cathederal Road, Cardiff; Mr Evan Evans, Rhondda Tea Warehouse, Tonypandy; Messrs W. and Sidney Miles, Treorchy; Mr Tom Rees Watkins; Mr and Mrs Radcliffe, Tonypandy; Gilfach cousins; Merthyr Vale cousins; Naunton, Cardiff (cousins); Cliff and Annie, Penygraig (cousins).

Revd J. Morgan (Llwynypia), assisted by the Revds E. Richards and D.C. Jones, officiated at the interment, which took place in the family vault. The office staff of Messrs Pughe-Jones and Davey; Messrs A.J. Williams, B. Jones, Walters, Evans, Rowlands, and Davies, acted as pall bearers. The funeral arrangements were carried out by Messrs J. Griffiths and Sons, Tonypandy.

Councillor Tom George

On Saturday afternoon on 28 January 1911, Councillor Tom George, the fourth Ferndale victim of the Hopkinstown disaster, was laid to rest at Ferndale Cemetery.

Above: Collapsed headstone at the grave of Mr Thomas George, buried at Ferndale Cemetery on 26 January 1911. (Ref. K68, uncon.)

Right: Broken headstone with details of Thomas George.

The cortege was an unusually long one, and covered a distance of around a mile in length. As the cortege proceeded along the route to the cemetery, large crowds stood in respectful silence whilst every blind in the town was drawn as a token of respect.

The procession was in the following order: Ministers of all the religious bodies, including the Revds B. Jones-Evans, MA, vicar of Ferndale; T. Davies, curate; John Davies, Briton Ferry, T. Lloyd, Ystrad; Emlyn Jones, Porth; M.H. Ellis, Trealaw; John Morgan, Llwynypia; W. Williams, Pontygwaith, Penrith; Thomas Trerhondda, T. Bryn Thomas Tabernacle, ? Thomas, Bethal; and Dr D.M. Phillips, Tylorstown.

Also there were members of the general public, members of the Lodge Committee, delegates of the Rhondda Miners' Monthly Meeting, members of the Rhondda Miners' District Committee, members of the Executive Council of the South Wales Miners' Federation, members of the local governing bodies, representatives of the Rhondda Labour and Liberal Association, Messrs Morris Morris and J. Kemp, Ynyshir; W. Lewis, Rhymney Valley; J. Lewis, Merthyr; J.D. Morgan, Swansea; W.E. Morgan, Anthracite District, and J. Winstone; the Ferndale Industrial Co-operative Society Ltd was represented by Messrs Tom Morgan, chairman; W.E. Emerson ME, vice chairman; Henry Davies, general manager; and James Jenkins, secretary; the Ferndale St John Ambulance Brigade, under the supervision of Supt Thos. H. Bufton ME; Ferndale Fire Brigade, Captain Walter Jones; members of the Rhondda District Council, including Councillors Ben Davies JP, chairman of the council; H.E. Maltby, D. Smith, J.D. Williams, Clydach Court; Daniel Evans and D.C. Evans and members of Glamorgan County Council; Mr T.W. Berry, director of education, and others.

The Penuel Chapel Choir, under the conductorship of Messrs John Thomas, checkweigher, W. Trevor Lewis, and Edward Rees, sang the following hymns on route to the cemetery: 'Sandon', 'Engedi', 'Builth', 'Lausanne', whilst 'Moab' was sung at the graveside during the interment.

The officiating minister was Revd B. Watkins, pastor of Penuel (CM), where the deceased had been a deacon. Mr Watkins referred in glowing terms to the excellent qualities of the deceased, and a warm tribute was also paid by Mr Owen Jenkins, senior deacon of Penuel Chapel.

Councillor Daniel Evans said that the position he was in that day was a very difficult one. It was not an easy thing to speak on the graveside of such a loyal friend as Tom George. He had worked with him both in public and private for a period of twelve years and had therefore many opportunities to form an opinion of the deceased. He agreed with him on almost every point in the working of the federation. He had always found him to be fair and someone who considered carefully both sides of a question. He remembered what was probably the last time Mr George spoke publicly, when the crisis of the last agreement among the miners loomed largely in the eyes of the public. As a member of the Conciliation Board, he thoroughly explained the position before the workmen and with courage backed by conviction he outlined to them a policy which was the means of saving the locality from disaster. He was never satisfied until his duty to his fellow workmen had been faithfully carried out.

Mr W. Brace, MP, followed and said it was a painful duty for him to say a word or two on this sad occasion. Tom George was his colleague on the Conciliation Board, and also on the Executive Council. He was one of nature's gentlemen, and a man who had placed on the altar of public service all he had possessed for the good of his fellow men. The three colleagues who had passed on were bosom friends. They were always together, and sat at the various conferences together, and it was said that they had been called upon to die together.

The coffin was lowered into the grave by members of the Ferndale Fire Brigade. The deceased's fellow deacons acted as bearers: Messrs John Howells, Regent Street, David Burnell, Duffryn Street, Owen Jenkins, Elm Street, J. Lloyd Evans, Aeron Street, J. Evans, Duffryn Street and John Thomas, checkweigher. The chief mourners were: Mrs George (widow); Misses Gladys, Gwennie and Morfydd George (daughters); Mr George George, Porth (brother); Mr and Mrs John George, Porth (brother and sister-in-law); Mr and Mrs William George, Aberdare (brother and sister-in-law); Mr and Mrs Thomas, Porth (brother-in-law and sister); Mr and Mrs Thomas Powell, Ferndale (brother-in-law and sister-in-law); Miss Edith Powell (niece); Mr and Mrs Evan Lewis, Pentre (brother-in-law and sister-in-law); Mr Richard Lewis, Cwmparc (brother-in-law); Messrs William Thomas, David John, and Lewis Lewis, Pentre (nephews); Mrs David Lewis and son, Cardiff (sister-in-law and nephew); Mrs Kate Lewis, Pentre (niece); Mr and Mrs William Thomas, Trecynon (nephew and niece); and Mr Tom Pugh, late of Mountain Ash (cousin).

Beautiful wreaths were sent by the following: the family of the deceased; Right Hon. LJ. Abraham, MP; 'Edward and Annie', Coity; Mre. Riley, Levenshulme, Manchester; Ferndale teachers; NUT; Llwynypia workmen; Ferndale Ambulance Brigade; Penuel Choir; the clerical staff of the Rhondda District Council; chief officials of the Rhondda District Council; Mrs E. Davies and family, Salisbury Hotel; Mr and Mrs D. Watts, Morgan; Rhonnda Miners' Federation; owners and workmen representing the Conciliation Board; a lady colleague on the Board of the Education Committee, Mrs Florence Nicholas; Ferndale Workman's Hall and Institute; Ferndale Checkweighers' Committee; and the Ferndale Federation Committee and workmen.

Excellent arrangements for the policing of the streets were carried out by police inspectors T.H. Thomas, Ferndale, and T. Williams, Porth, and police sergeants T. Richards and Shelly.

Councillor William H. Morgan

On Saturday 28 January 1911, upper Rhondda was in deep mourning when the body of the late Councillor William Herbert Morgan was conveyed to its last resting place at Treorchy Cemetery. The attendance at this funeral was so great that the cortege extended for over a mile in length, and was representative of all levels of the community. Blinds were drawn at all business premises and private houses on the route to the cemetery. Thousands of people lined the streets in which the procession would pass in order to pay their last respects to a great public man whom they held in such high esteem.

Revd H. Harris, DO (Treherbert) officiated at the house and the service was very impressive and exceedingly moving, particularly when the Libanus Chapel Choir sang the old Welsh hymn, 'Yn y dyffroedcy maur a'r tonau'.

In addition to the family carriages, many more followed the cortege to the cemetery. The order of the carriages ran as follows:

First: Mrs W.H. Morgan (widow); Mrs Watts Morgan, Porth; Mrs Margaret Jones, Swansea; Mrs J. Morgan, Treherbert; Miss M. Morgan, Miss Dock, and Master Kimberley Morgan.

Second: Mrs Morgan James, Hafod; Mrs Morgan, Treforest; Mrs U. Davies, Ynyshir; Mrs D. Davies, Ynyshir; Mrs Tim Davies, Ferndale; Mrs Enoch Davies, Swansea; and Master Harry Davies.

Third: Miss Bertha Davies, Ynyshir; Misses Bloduen, Elsie, Arianwen and Liluen Jones, Swansea; Miss M.A. Davies, Ynyshir; and Doris, Swansea.

Fourth: Miss Lucy Davies, Treherbert; Mrs M.A. Thomas, Treorchy; Mrs Rachel Thomas, Ynyshir; Mrs William Davies, Treherbert; Mrs James James, Senghenydd; and Mr Charles Davies, Merthyr.

Fifth: - ? -, Mr J.A. James, Treharris, and two daughters, Mrs W. Davies, Cwmbach, and Mrs Rees Walters, Ynyshir.

Sixth: Miss J. Phillips, Taffs Well, Miss Robson, Taffs Well, Miss M.A. Mirts, Swansea, Mrs Emily Thomas, Swansea, Mrs B. Price, Swansea, and Mrs E. Eddmunds, Swansea.

Seventh: Miss M. Jones, Treherbert; Miss Walters, Treherbert; Miss Jones, Treherbert; Miss James, Treherbert; Miss R.A. Davies, Treherbert.

Eighth: Mrs Whiting, Treherbert; Mrs M. Lloyd, Blaenrhondda; Mrs Tom Davies, Treherbert; Miss S. Jones, Ferndale; Mrs E. Jones, Ferndale; Mrs Lewis Davies, Merthyr; and Mrs Ted Thomas, Swansea.

The following mourners were on foot: Mr John Morgan (brother); Mr W. Davies, Treherbert (cousin); Mr W. Davies, Ynysyhir (brother-in-law); Mr Tim Davies, Ferndale (brother-in-law); Mr Enoch Davies, Swansea (brother-in-law); Messrs Wm. Bevan, Brigend and W. Morgan, Treforest (cousins); Messrs James James, Senghenydd; Lewis James, Ammanford; and David James, Senghenydd (cousins); Messrs James Davies, Treherbert; Glyn Davies, Ynyshir;

Family grave of William H. Morgan buried at Treorchy Cemetary
on 28 January 1911. (Ref. T2/9)

David Gover, Ynyshir; David Thos. Jones, Swansea; and Oswald Jones, Swansea
(cousins); Messrs Enoch Davies, Treorchy; John Kinsey, Cardiff; Jack Kinsey,
Cardiff; Bert Kinsey, Cardiff; Atchie Kinsey, Cardiff; Handel Williams, Cardiff;
Tudor Jenkins, Swansea; A. Siminster, Treorchy; Tommy Davies, Treherbert; Owen
Davies, Treherbert; John Hurlo J., Cardiff; and Captain J.R.L. Williams, Cardiff.

The South Wales Miners' Federation Executive was represented by Messrs
T. Richards MP, Alfred Onions JP, Hubert Jenkins, W. Vyce, D. Morgan, T. Lucas
and J. Manning, whilst the Rhondda District of Miners was represented by
Messrs Watts Morgan, L.R. Thomas (chairman of district), and John Jones

(treasurer); and the District Committee by Messrs W. John, T. Smith and others representing the Cambrian workmen, whilst most of the Lodges in the district were represented.

The following were also present: Dr W.E. Thomas; Revd Canon Lewis, RD; Mr Leonard Llewellyn (general manager of the Cambrian Combine); Mr Hedley Clark (sub-agent, Glamorgan Colliery); Mr T.D. Lawrence, (of Cambrian Combine); Mr W.O. Wight (agent Messrs Cory Bros.); Mr J. Rowland (representing Mr D. Lloyd George); Mr H.J. Abraham (representing the Right Hon. Wm. Abraham MP); Mr W.P. Nicholas (clerk of Rhondda District Council); Alderman E.H. Davies; Councillor E.T. Davies; Councillor Enoch Davies, JP; Councillors W.T. Jones, D.R. Jones, ME; W. Thomas; W.P. Thomas; James James; Griffith Evans; Walter Williams; Edward Jones; Tom Jones (Treorchy); Messrs David Williams, Tom Thomas, T. Willams (Tydraw Collieries); Dr John James (director of education, Cardiff); Revds E. Richards (Tonypandy), W. Cynon Evans (Treherbert); J. Pethian Davies; J.T. Jones; W. Morris, DO; Messrs J. Samuel, D.J. Charles (Pontypridd); Silas Jenkins (headmaster, Blsenrhondda); T. Jones (headmaster, Dunraven); D. James (headmaster, Treherbert); B. Gabe (headmaster, Penrenglyn); John Howells (headmaster, Ton); Howell Howells (headmaster, Treorchy); U.R. Edwards (headmaster, Bodringallt); Llew. Davies (headmaster, Pentre); Miss M.E. Adams (headmistress, Treherbert); Dr J.D. Jenkins (medical officer of health); Mr U.J. Jones (surveyor); Mr Dan Davies, and Guardians William Eveleigh and Evan Watkins (Treherbert).

Floral tributes: forty-five wreaths covered the coffin, the hearse and another carriage. At the foot of the coffin was a wreath from the chairman and members of the Rhondda District Council, and at the head was a pillow of violets and white flowers from Mrs W.P. Nicholas. Wreaths were also sent by: 'The Sorrowing Widow'; 'John, Martha and Family'; 'Maggie and Family'; 'Arianwen, Lilwen and Doris'; the brothers-in-law; 'Gwladys, Irene, Edward, and Myfanwy'; Rhondda Miners' Federation; Joint Conciliation Board of South Wales Coal Trade; chairman and directors of Fernhill Colliery; manager and officials of Fernhill Colliery; and North Dunraven workmen and Fernhill Institute members; 'John and Dai'; chief officials of Rhondda District Council; clerical staff of Rhondda District Council; teachers of Dunraven Council Schools; staff of Blaenrhondda Council Schools; Right Hon. William Abraham, MP; Mr and Mrs D. Watts Morgan, Dr Grant, Maerdy; Mrs Austin and Nurse Jones; 'Lydia, David, and Pollie'; Mr and Mrs J. Ryan; Conductor and few friends of Libanus Chapel Choir; Committee of Ton Co-operative Society; Treherbert employees of Ton Co-operative Society; boy and girl friends; Mr and Mrs D.P. Beam, Swansea; Mr William M. Thomas, Kilgerran; Mr Thomas Davies and family, Treherbert; teachers of Treherbert Council Schools; teachers of Penyrenglyn Council Schools; Rhondda and Pontypridd Teachers Association; Mr and Mrs

Headstone details of William
Herbert Morgan.

David Williams, Ynyswen; Miss Bessie Price, Swansea; Mr and Mrs Watkin Price,
Treherbert; Mr Thomas Evan Jones, solicitor, Cardiff; Dr and Mrs W.C. Hinde,
Treherbert; Treherbert Trades and Labour Council, Treherbert Co-operative
Committee; Mid-Rhondda strikers and two tributes were anonymous.

On behalf of the Executive Council of the South Wales Miners' Federation, Mr
Onions spoke at the graveside, and paid a glowing tribute to his dead colleague. He
wished to press home the fact that Mr W.H. Morgan was not a traitor to the men,
and he warned them to be careful in choosing his successor. Mr Morgan's loss
would be a severe one, and would cause almost irreparable damage to the
federation. A gentleman by nature, he was also a man of culture. To the widow and
sorrowing relatives he tendered the most profound condolence of the Miners'
Federation.

Dr Harris also added an eloquent tribute in Welsh.

Unmarked grave of Mr
George Gould buried at
Cathay's Cemetery Cardiff
on 29 March 1911.
(Ref. S. 3327)

Mr George Gould.

The funeral of Mr George Gould, Treherbert Street, Cardiff, took place on Wednesday 29 March 1911, with the deceased being interred at Cathays Cemetery, Cardiff. Mr Gould had been the guard on the mineral train involved in the disaster on the Taff Vale Railway at Pontypridd; he received severe injuries in the collision and eventually passed away on Saturday 25 March 1911 at the Cardiff Infirmary.

The greatest sympathy was manifested on all sides, and many hundreds of mourners in addition to the railway employees, were present at the cemetery to pay a tribute to one who was highly respected in the Cathays Ward and extremely popular among his fellow workers.

The coffin was borne from the house to the cemetery chapel, and then to the grave by Taff Vale employees. Revd W.G. Howells, Pastor of the Cathays Presbyterian Church, officiated in the chapel and also performed the last sad rites at the graveside.

The chief mourners were the widow and the three daughters, and among others present were representatives of the local branches of the Amalgamated Society of Railway Servants and the Cathays Liberal Club, both of which organisations sent wreaths, and Charles Hughes of the Taff Vale Railway Traffic department represented the railway company.

Mourning the Dead.

Funeral of Disaster Victims

Remarkable Street Scenes.

Touching Tributes.

The victims of the Taff Vale train disaster were laid to rest last week amid scenes of pathos which could not leave one unmoved. From a spectacular standpoint the large funerals—particularly those of the three dead Councillors—will live long in the public memory, while all around there were deep and sincere signs of widespread sympathy.

From *Rhondda Leader*, Thursday 26 January 1911.

five

The Inquest

The Victims

The inquest for the victims of the Hopkinstown railway disaster was opened at the police station, Pontypridd on Thursday morning, 26 January 1911, by Coroner Mr R.J. Rhys, Aberdare, into the circumstances leading to the deaths of the eleven victims.

The members of the jury were: Foreman, Mr Edward Williams, Messrs J. Brooks, ? Davies, Thomas Jones (Pontypridd Ironmongery Co.), R. Williams (ironmonger), J. Phillips (hosier), ? Evans, David Richards (Llanover Arms), Thomas Jeremey, Gomer Thomas, E.L. Thomas, Jon Delany, William Johnson (Parade), Gwilym Evans and Thomas Morgan (fruiterer). Lt-Col Druitt represented the Board of Trade, whilst the Taff Vale Railway Company were represented by Mr A. Beasley, general manager, Mr T.E. Harland, traffic manager, and Mr Oscar Hurford, stationmaster, Pontypridd.

Others present were Mr W.P. Nicholas, for the families of councillors W.H. Morgan, Tom George, and Tom Harries, and also Edward Lewis. Mr D. Watts Morgan attended for the South Wales Miners' Federation, Mr J.H. Thomas MP for the Amalgamated Society of Railway Servants, Mr H.H. Parfitt for the Locomotive Enginemen's Association, Messrs Jones Pughe and Davey for the relatives of Margaret Elizabeth Davies, Alderman W.R. Davies for the relatives of Revd W. Landeg Powell, and Mr Idris Price for the relatives of Hannah Jenkins.

The coroner said that he had been a coroner for many years, but this was the first occasion that he had to deal with a case of this sort. When they considered the number of railways in the district and the amount of traffic and the congestion caused, with the necessity of running trains at short intervals, and working under adverse circumstances, they could consider it fortunate that they had not had similar accidents before.

He only proposed to take evidence of identification that day, and to adjourn the proceedings until such a day as would meet the convenience of the majority of those concerned. The loss of life was very serious, but he was one of those persons who looked upon one death as of the same importance as fifty. He desired to express his deepest sympathy with the relatives of the victims and the sufferers. When one knew those who were among the dead, it brought the whole thing near home.

Whilst some of the victims were only school children, others were men who had obtained a degree of prominence in the industrial world. He knew councillors W.H. Morgan and Tom George well, and regretted their deaths very much. Mr A. Beasley, general manager of the Taff Vale Railway Company, said he was present to express on behalf of the chairman and directors of the Taff Vale Railway, and every member of the executive staff, including himself, their deep regret at the occurrence, and he desired to express his deepest and heartfelt sympathy with the relatives and sufferers. Regarding the injured at the Cardiff Infirmary, he had just received the following message from that institution: 'Injured persons in infirmary progressing satisfactorily, house surgeon hopes they will all pull through'.

It was the desire of those whom he represented, Mr Beasley continued, that the whole of the facts should be ascertained, and the cause of the calamity brought out. The company would give the jury every possible assistance to enable them to arrive at a just conclusion.

In the meantime he said that the Taff Vale Railway Company unreservedly admitted full responsibility for the accident, and that the whole of the claims arising out of the accident would be promptly met, with due regard to the circumstances of each case.

Lt-Col Druitt, on behalf of the Board of Trade, said he desired to associate himself with the sentiments already expressed. The President of the Board of Trade had sent him a message expressing his deepest sympathy to the relatives of those killed or injured, and also with the Miners' Federation in the loss they had sustained.

Mr J.H. Thomas MP, of the Amalgamated Society of Railway Servants, also associated himself with everything that had been said. Some of those killed were personal friends of his. As a railway man taking part in the proceedings, he could assure the bereaved that the employees of the company would render every assistance to ascertain facts.

Mr H. Parfitt, organising secretary of the Locomotive Enginemen and Firemen's Association also expressed his sympathy with the relatives of the victims and the injured. Mr W.P. Nicholas said he desired to thank all who had spoken for their kind expression of sympathy and also the President of the Board of Trade for his sympathy with the Miners' Federation Union.

Identification of the Victims

Evidence of identification of the victims was given as follows:

Councillor Tom George, aged fifty-eight, by his brother-in-law, Mr Thomas Powell, 64 Duffryn Street, Ferndale.

Councillor W.H. Morgan, aged forty-four, by his brother-in-law, Mr Davies, Ynyshir.

Councillor Tom Harries, aged thirty-nine, by his brother-in-law, Mr John Davies, 99 Madeline Street, Pontygwaith.

Miss Margaret Davies, aged ten, by her father Mr Jack Davies, Commercial Hotel, Ferndale.

Mr Thomas John Hodges, aged thirty-four, and his son Thomas Ivor, aged nine, by his brother-in-law, Mr James Edward Price, Ferndale.

Revd W. Landeck Powell, aged sixty, by his brother-in-law, County Councillor James Evans, Cambrian House Clydach Vale.

Miss Hannah Jenkins, aged sixteen, by her father, Mr Edward Jenkins, Morgan Street, Trehafod.

Mr Edward Lewis, aged thirty-nine, by a friend from Pontypridd, Mr W.J. Schoufield.

Mr Idris I.M. Evans, aged eighteen, by his uncle, Dr Idris Morgan, Llwynypia.

Mr Lodwig Hughes, aged thirty-seven, by his brother-in-law, Mr Thomas Howells, 33 James Street, Maerdy.

Dr John M. MacDonald, Hopkinstown, gave evidence on the injuries and said that the cause of death in the majority of cases was attributed to fractured skulls, whilst others died from shock and suffocation.

The Coroner: I take it that in nearly all the cases death was either instantaneous or the injuries which caused death produced insensibility at once?

Dr MacDonald: Yes, sir.

The Coroner: None of them lingered at all?

Dr MacDonald: I don't think so, sir.

The Coroner: I am glad to hear that.

The proceedings were then adjourned until 10 a.m. on the next Thursday, 31 January 1911.

Inquest Disclosures

The inquest on the disaster was resumed on Thursday 31 January 1911, at Pontypridd Police Court, with Coroner Mr R.J. Rhys, Aberdare, in attendance together with Lt-Col Druitt, of the Board of Trade, Mr A. Beasley, general manager of the Taff Vale Railway, Mr H.M. Ingledew, representing the Taff Vale Railway Company, Mr J.H. Thomas MP, appearing for the Amalgamated Society of Railway Servants, Mr W.P. Nicholas and Mr Watts Morgan for the Miners' Federation, together with Mr W.R. Davies, Mr Davey (of Jones-Pughe and Davey), Mr H. Thomas, Aberdare, and Mr Idris Price for the relatives of the deceased.

The coroner, addressing the jury, stated that he proposed to call witnesses to approve a plan of the section of the railway where the accident occurred. The plan would show them the position of the signal boxes and the signals that operated from them, and they would have to carry these carefully in their minds so that they might know how the signalmen did their work and how the signals were given, received, and recorded.

The police and magistrates court, now demolished, which had been used for the inquest on the tragedy.

Mr W.J. Edwards, the chief assistant engineer of the TVR, produced a large wall plan showing the railway lines from the Gyfeillion lower cabin to the lower Rhondda signal box, and explained that the curve between them where the accident occurred was 35 chain radius (770 yards). The head of the train that went into the mineral train was on the straight, and the mineral train seemed to have been driven down 45ft after the accident.

The Coroner: The marks of the wheels on the sleepers were very distinct, and you can see where the mineral guard's van was brought to rest.
The Witness: There is no doubt about the position.
The Coroner: Would that van be round the curve when it was sighted by the passenger train?
The Witness: It would be round the curve when the driver sighted it properly.

In reply to further questions, the witness explained that there were ten lines of rails at the spot, of which three were up lines and three down lines.

The Coroner: It seems to me very difficult to realise on what pair of rails the van was running, and that the driver of the passenger train might be confused. Do you know anything about the condition of the signals? Were all the means of communication between the various boxes in perfect working order?

The Witness: They were.

The Coroner: Any suggestion of any difficulty in any of the signal apparatus?

The Witness: None whatever.

Signal Arrangements Explained

Mr Thomas Edward Harland, the next witness called, explained the signalling arrangements, and in reply to the coroner said that all the principal signals were recorded by the signalman.

The Coroner: What is rule 55, Mr Harland?

The Witness: This is a safety rule which the men on a train are required to observe so as to guard against any oversight on the part of the signalman. The effect of the rule is this: that immediately a train comes to a standstill at the signal, the fireman, or some other person, has to go to the signal box, and remain with the signalman until the train can go ahead.

The Coroner: It is really to keep two minds to work instead of one?

The Witness: Yes.

Mr Harland then further stated that these rules were brought to the notice of their employees, every man receiving a copy when he entered the company's service, and signing for it.

Mr J.H. Thomas: You explained to the jury that when certain signals are given the indicator moves and shows the position of the instrument. When the signalman at the Rhondda Cutting gives 'Line clear' for a passenger train, would the needle in the Gyfeillon Lower Box move?

The Witness: It would be shown in the register kept by the signalman.

Mr Thomas was proceeding to ask further questions, when the coroner intimated that Mr Harland would be recalled for questioning at a later stage.

The next witness called was Mr Albert Edward Hutchings, Glynfach, Porth, who had been a signalman for ten years. He had worked at this box for five months before the day of the accident. He had come on duty at nine o'clock that morning. The relief signalman, Mr Phillip James Dipper, remained in the box with him until the accident occurred. He stated that the first train he took from the Gyfeillon upper box was an engine and mineral train, and was accepted by the Rhondda cutting at 9.23 a.m., and received the signal 'train out of section' from the latter at 9.30 a.m. That meant that he could accept another train. The next signal he received was for a passenger train, which was offered to him by Gyfeillon upper at 9.43 a.m. He informed Rhondda cutting, and they accepted at the same time. He received the signal 'train on line' from Gyfeillon pper, the train entering his section at 9.37 a.m. and passed the box at 9.48 a.m.

After further questions by the coroner, the witness stated that after accepting the signal 'train on line', he received a 'blocking back' signal, and, having a passenger train passing at that time, felt alarmed. Due to the position of the levers in the signal box, and realising the danger, he had no time to set the advance distant signal against it, realising that the passenger train was travelling at approximately 35mph. He did, however, rush as quickly as possible to the signal levers and put them on danger, but as the passenger train was passing the signal box when he received the signal he realised it was too late.

The next witness, Mr Sidney Quick, who had been a signalman for thirty-two years, and had been employed at the Rhondda cutting for the last five years, stated that on the day of the accident he commenced his duties at 8.00 a.m. The passenger train involved in the accident was due at 9.52 a.m., and he was positive that he had no trains handed to him between the passenger train at 9.50 a.m. and that which was due at 9.52 a.m.

Inspector Tuck came into the signal box and after a short while a fireman came in, who gave the position of his train, stating that it was on the No.1 line and held up. The witness immediately blocked the line, and stated that this was the first indication he had of a mineral train being on the No.1 line.

The coroner was concerned that this incident was not recorded in the record book (standard procedure), together with some other anomalies which had occurred between the signalman and the fireman in the time lapse due to the signalman having a discussion with Inspector Tuck.

The next witness, George Lewis, Treorchy Street, Cathays, Cardiff, a locomotive fireman, stated that on the morning of the accident he was on engine No.121 pulling the mineral train from the Lewis Merthyr Colliery. The train was made up of forty-three trucks and a goods van. They stopped at the Rhondda cutting because the signal was against them and before they came to a standstill the whistle was put on.

The engine had not been fully lubricated that morning and when they came to a standstill, he said, he had continued with his lubricating duties, which took around five or six minutes (implementation of Rule 55, which states that lubrication does not take place whilst the train is in motion). [This was found to be unsatisfactory due to short stops.]

During this time the engine driver was watching for the signal to proceed, and as the signal was given, he (Mr Lewis) went towards the signal box at the Rhondda cutting. When he moved to the door to report, he found that Inspector Tuck and the signalman were in conversation, which lasted for approximately two minutes, before the signalman spoke to him enquiring what line he was on.

The signalman then stated that he had no knowledge of the mineral train being there, but with the passenger train approaching gave him the signal to continue.

The witness was closely questioned by the coroner as to the time in getting from the engine to the signal box, the witness stating that he had not wasted any time on the journey to the box.

This was corroborated by the next witness, Mr Andrew Davison, of Spencer Street, Cardiff, the driver of engine No.121.

The coroner closely questioned him regarding his fireman, who had been carrying out lubrication duties during the five minutes' wait, instead of proceeding immediately to the signal box. The witness stated that there was nothing he could do, as he had to wait for the signal, and as there was at that time another train passing he knew that the signal could not be lowered for him because a train was on No.3 line. This was the reason why he did not insist that the fireman went immediately to the signal box.

The next witness, Mr Alexander Sellars, the driver of the passenger train, stated that the automatic vacuum brakes on the train were in good order, and when he passed the Gyfeillon lower box he was travelling at around 30mph (at that point the maximum speed was 35mph). He had shut off steam after passing over the level crossing near the Great Western Colliery, as he had enough in reserve to carry him through to Pontypridd Station.

His fireman was the first to observe the obstruction ahead of him and shouted to him (the driver) to 'Whoa Up'. He was in the act at that time of applying the brakes as he had seen the train when he was approximately thirty-five to forty yards from it. He remained at his post, applying the brakes until the engine ran into the back of the mineral train. He stated that had he received sufficient warning he would have been able to apply both the vacuum and the steam brakes sooner, which would have reduced the force of impact, or possibly avoided the collision altogether.

This was then corroborated by the fireman, Mr John Jones.
Further evidence relating to the crash was given by Mr John White, guard, and Mr Thomas Goodwin, brakesman, in charge of the passenger train.

The Coroner Sums Up
The coroner, in his summing up, reviewed the evidence at length. In his opinion there was no question that the signalmen were overworked and tired, but it appeared that circumstances which occurred around the time the two trains were in their respective positions prior to the impact was the main cause of the accident. He realised that confusion caused by other traffic having to be dealt with at the same

time could only add to the problem and be part of the reason that mistakes were made.

If Mr Quick had received the signal for the mineral train, and did not record it, and then accepted the passenger train before the mineral train had passed his signal box, something that he would have had to have done in order to clear his section, he (the coroner) could not understand how such an experienced man could have done such a thing.

It was for the jury to decide if they were to put the blame for the collision on Mr Quick, or from earlier evidence given, believe that Mr Hutchings had given him the signal for the mineral train which he had accepted, and then had accepted the passenger train before his section had been cleared.

He stated that it was for the jury to decide from the evidence given whether blame should be attached to anyone, or, if they felt the evidence was unclear, to bring in an open verdict. It was a very difficult position for them to decide upon.

The Verdict

The jury retired at 3.55 p.m. to consider the verdict, and after deliberating for a time handed a written verdict to the coroner at 5.15 p.m. This stated that the deaths of the unfortunate victims was due to a collision between a passenger and mineral train, through a misunderstanding in signalling procedure, but owing to the conflicting nature of the evidence they were unable to fix the blame on anyone.

They wished, however, to pass a strong vote of censure on driver Davison, of the mineral train, in as much as he neglected to comply with Rule 55 to send his fireman to inform the signal box of the fact that he had been held up and detained above the signal for a space of time.

The coroner accepted the verdict and closed the inquest.

The Official Verdict

In the official report on the disaster, compiled by Lt-Col Druitt RE, on 5 April 1911, among his recommendations was that more could have been done by the guard of the mineral train (Mr George Gould) whilst waiting for authorisation to proceed, by observing that the signal procedure was being carried out. If the check had been implemented in this instance, as recommended in Rule 55, then there was the possibility that by observing the discrepancy of the signal procedure he could have laid detonators on the line and possibly have avoided the collision that took place between the two trains, with such tragic results.

Shown is a brief account of the report, with full details of the recommendations of Lt-Col Druitt RE.

The Official Report on the TVR Disaster of 23 January 1911

Important Recommendations

This report was issued on Wednesday the 5th. April 1911, on the fatal collision which occurred on the 23rd January 1911, between a passenger train and a mineral train at the Coke Ovens, Nr. Pontypridd on the Taff Vale Railway. Eleven Passengers were killed, four passengers and the guard of the mineral were seriously injured, the guard has since died of his injuries, and seventeen passengers complained of minor injuries or shock, and a passenger brakes man was also slightly injured.

The collision took place on the No.1 down line (down main line) in the block section between the Gyfeillon Lower and the Rhondda Cutting Junction signal cabins and was due to irregular block workings between these two cabins.

In reviewing the evidence, it must be borne in mind that the clock in the Rhondda cutting junction cabin was three minutes faster than that at the Gyfeillion lower cabin.

In order to simplify the report, three minutes have been deducted in all cases from the times recorded by the signalman in his train register book at the Rhondda cutting junction, to bring it in line with the clock at the Gyfeillion lower cabin, which I have taken as the standard. The difference in the clocks is accounted for by the fact that the signalman gets a correct time sent to them daily at 10:00 a.m., and the collision occurred shortly before that time.

It must further be noted that the block telegraph instruments in use on the Taff Vale Railway are those known as Tyer's two-position single-wire block telegraph instruments, in which the indicators have only two positions, 'Train Arrived' and 'Train on Line', and the normal position of the indicators when the block instruments are not in use is at 'Train Arrived'.

The signalmen concerned were Albert Hutchings at Gyfeillion lower, and Sidney Quick at Rhondda cutting; and at the time of the collision there was also a relief signalman (Dipper) and a groundsman (Machant) in Gyfeillion lower cabin.

Dipper stated that he did not remember Hutchings' section signal for the mineral train on the No.1 sending the 'Entering Down Line', and he did not hear that signal being acknowledged by Quick, nor the 'Out of Section' signal being sent for the train.

A Probable Solution

If Dipper is correct, a likely explanation for the mistake (although not necessarily the correct one) is that after Hutchings had offered the 'Is Line Clear' signal for the mineral train, and had it accepted by Quick at 9.23 a.m. on No.1 line, he omitted to send the 'Entering Section' signal for it, and so, of course Quick could not have acknowledged that signal, and did not move the indicators of the block instruments to the 'Train On Line' position. Quick must have omitted to enter in his train register the times he received and acknowledged the 'Is Line Clear' signal for the mineral train, if these signals were readily transmitted.

Six minutes later, at 9.29 a.m., Hutchings sent the 'Is Line Clear' signal for the Barry train on No.3 Line. Quick acknowledged this at once, and the train proceeded, and Quick sent the 'Out of Section' signal for it at 9.36 a.m. (Gyfeillion lower time).

Hutchings probably took this Out of Section signal to apply to the first train, i.e. the mineral train on No.1 down line, as he had entered that time, 9.36 a.m., and of receiving the 'Out of Section' signal for the Barry train at 9.39 a.m., because he thought he must have sent and received them respectively. There is little doubt but that the entries were made before the collision occurred, as Hutchings was too much upset by the occurrence to do so afterwards.

Important Recommendations

In summing up, Colonel Druitt pointed out that there was a heavy mixed traffic on many sections of the Taff Vale Railway, and that he trusted that the company would consider the advisability of replacing the two-position instruments with others of an improved pattern with three positions for the indicator, for the passenger line, as the opportunity occurred.

He went on:
With such a sudden stop as the passenger train made after the collision it seems to me that some of the vehicles of the train must be severely damaged. But I understand that consideration is being given by railway companies to the question how, if possible, the serious telescoping of one carriage into another, owing to the frames sliding over each other, may be avoided.

The time required for a guard to satisfy himself that a fireman has gone to the signal box and then return to his van before the train can proceed must be very considerable, and it seems to me that a guard of such a train would be better employed in looking out behind him, especially as in many cases when delays occur the block sections are short and the signals behind would be visible to him.

Certainly in this case the guard of the mineral train, who remained in his van, had he looked could have seen the signals off for the passenger train at 9.43 a.m., five minutes before the collision occurred, as his van was only forty yards ahead of the advance starter, and 110 yards ahead of the starting signal, and he would have had time to have gone back and laid down detonators on the line and warn the passenger train of the obstruction ahead, even if he could not have got to the Gyfeillion Lower signal cabin.

Note: From the statement made by the coroner, and the findings and the recommendations of the Independent Arbitrator, in our judgement is there one or perhaps more persons to blame, or was it the circumstances of events which results in a combination of errors at that particular time which resulted in the unfortunate disaster?

SATURDAY, FEBRUARY 4, 1911

The T.V.R. Crash

Inquest Disclosures.

Fatal Signalling Misunderstanding.

Sensational Evidence.

Jury Censure Engine Driver.

Some sensational evidence was given at the resumed inquest on the eleven victims of the Taff Vale Railway smash, which was held at Pontypridd Police Court on Tuesday last. Occupying a seat on the Bench with the Coroner (Mr. R. J. Rhys, Aberdare) were Lieut.-Colonel Druitt, of the Board of Trade, and Mr. A. Beasley, general manager of the Taff Vale Railway. Mr. H. M. Ingledew represented the Taff Vale Railway Company; Mr. J. H. Thomas, M.P., appeared for the Amalgamated Society of Railway Servants; Mr. W. P. Nicholas and Mr. Watts Morgan for the Miners' Federation; and Mr. W. R. Davies, Mr. Davey (Jones-Pughe and Davey), Mr. H. Thomas, Aberdare, and Mr. Idris Price for the relatives of the deceased.

The Coroner, addressing the jury, said he proposed first of all calling witnesses

Left: From *Rhondda Leader,* Saturday 4 February 1911.

Below: From *Rhondda Leader,* Thursday 26 January 1911.

Inquest Opened at Pontypridd.

Railway Company Accepts Full Responsibility.

Coroner and Railway Accidents.

Wonder It had not happened before.

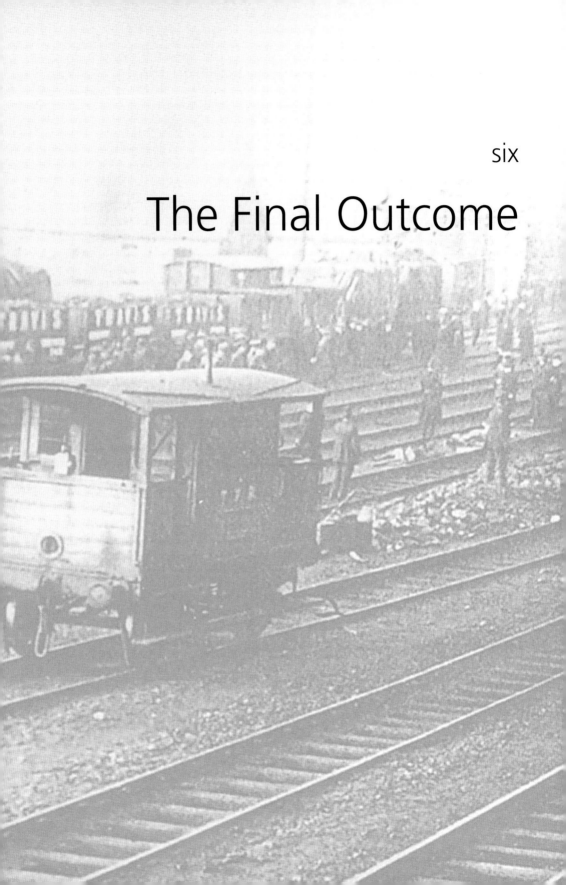

six

The Final Outcome

Damage and Compensation Claims

After the coroner's verdict, damages were received by the relatives of the deceased, and by the persons who had been injured by the disaster. These damages were claimed under common law against the Taff Vale Railway. Although the exact amounts received were not published, one would have expected that they would have taken into consideration the circumstances in which the dependants of those whom had died were left, together with the severity of the injuries of those who had survived.

Like today, any large company – and the Taff Vale Railway organisation was a large company – would go to any lengths to protect the interests of their shareholders. This can be seen in the only details available on damages given to Miss Hannah Jenkins, of Morgan Street, Trehafod, aged sixteen. She had only been on the train barely ten minutes when she met her death. It was argued that because she was only a milliner's apprentice, and not bringing in any wages to her parents, and therefore not contributing monies to the family home, it was considered no damages should be paid to her parents. Her parents appealed against this decision claiming damages under Lord Campbell's Fatal Accidents Act, 1848, for the death of their daughter as the result of an accident on the Taff Vale Railway.

Judgement was given by Mr Justice Channell, who awarded damages of £50 to Mr Jenkins and £25 to his wife.

In October of that year the Taff Vale Railway Company appealed to the House of Lords to overturn this judgement. After much deliberation the appeal was rejected and Mr and Mrs Jenkins received the monies due to them.

If this is an indication of the attitude of the company in assessing the amount of damages to the other victims, it was of little wonder that the families of those involved tried other means in which to obtain extra finance under the new Workmen's Compensation Act of that time.

In February of that year, the Deacons of Pisgah CM Chapel, Penygraig, received a communication from Mr W.R. Davies, solicitor, Pontypridd, claiming compensation on behalf of the family of Revd W. Landeck Powell, of Caerphilly, as the latter had met his death when returning home from his Sunday engagement at the chapel.

No further information is available on the outcome of this claim, but it may have been influenced by the important decision given by His Honour Judge Bryn Roberts at Pontypridd County Court in October of that year, in the case of George *versus* South Wales Miners' federation.

The Court Case

Present at the county court, which was presided over by His Honour Judge Bryn Roberts, were Mr A. T. James (instructed by Messrs Morgan, Bruce, and Nicholas, solicitors) who appeared for the applicants, and Mr Llewellyn Williams MP (instructed by Mr G.F. Forsdike, Cardiff) who represented the respondents.

Mr James explained that these proceedings were in connection with a claim made by the widow of the late Councillor Thomas George, Ferndale, for payment of compensation in respect to his death. The deceased was one of the unfortunate victims of the collision on the Taff Vale Railway at Pontypridd. At the time of his death he, along with the late councillors W.H. Morgan and T. Harries, who were also killed and were members of the Executive Council of the South Wales Miners' Federation, who were in fact in the ill-fated train on their way to London to transact federation business. Mr James then stated that he would also be representing the other councillors at a later stage in claiming compensation.

However, it would appear that under the articles laid down under the Workman's Compensation Act the wording stipulated that claimants were not entitled to recover both damages and compensation.

As the applicant(s) had already recovered damages from the Taff Vale Railway Company, they were therefore precluded from also recovering compensation under this Act.

After much discussion between the representatives of both parties, Mr James contended that he was entitled to recover the funeral expenses even though his Honour Judge Bryn Roberts had found against him in terms of compensation. His Honour stated that he could not allow the recovery of the funeral expenses, which, after all, was really compensation. He therefore found for the respondents, and made certain allowances in regard to costs.

The court was then adjourned.

Note:

No further information has been made available to indicate whether any of the other families of the deceased, or indeed those who were injured had made a claim under this Act. In all probability they were awaiting the outcome of this court case, and realised that they would be unsuccessful in any claim due to the judge's ruling.

A selection of newspaper clippings illustrating
the reactions to the inquest and its findings

Below: From *Pontypridd Observer*, 4 February 1911.

INQUEST ON RAILWAY VICTIMS.

PRACTICALLY AN OPEN VERDICT.

WHO'S TO BLAME?

Mr. R. J. Rhys, Aberdare (District Coroner)
conducted the adjourned enquiry at the Pontypridd Police Court into the circumstances attending the death of the eleven victims of the terrible
disaster on the T.V.R.

Lieutenant-colonel Druitt appeared for the
Board of Trade, whilst the Taff Vale Railway
Company were represented by Mr. H. M. Ingle-
dew, Mr. A. Beasley, general manager, Mr. T. E.
Harland, traffic manager, and Mr. Oscar Hurford,
stationmaster, Pontypridd.

Others present were Mr. W. P. Nicholas for
the families of Councillors W. H. Morgan, Tom
George, and Tom Harris, and Edward Lewis;
Mr. D. Watts Morgan for the South Wales Miners'
Federation; Mr. J. H. Thomas, M.P., for the
Amalgamated Society of Railway Servants;
Mr. H. H. Parfitt, the Locomotive Enginemen's
Association; Mr. Davey (of Messrs. Jones,
Pughe, and Davey), for the relatives of Margaret
Elizabeth Davies; Alderman W. R. Davies for
the relatives of the Rev. Landeg Powell; Mr.
Idris Price for the relatives of Hannah Jenkins
and Mr. H. Thomas; and Mr. W. Thomas,
solicitor, for the South Wales Enginemen's Asso-
ciation, on behalf of Mrs. Lodwig Hughes. Cap-
tain Lindsay, the chief-constable, and Deputy-
chief-constable Cole were also in attendance.

THE VERDICT

The jury, after an hour's absence, returned the following verdict:—

We come to the conclusion that the deaths of the unfortunate victims of this appalling disaster were caused by the passenger train colliding with a mineral train through a misunderstanding in signalling, but, owing to the conflicting evidence submitted, the jury find themselves unable to place the blame on either individual signalman.

Above: From *Pontypridd Observer*, 4 February 1911.

Below: From *Rhondda Leader*, 25 February 1911.

Echo of the T.V.R. Collision

Penygraig Chapel Asked to Pay Compensation.

On Friday, the deacons of Pisgah (C.M.) Church, Penygraig, received a communication from Mr. W. R. Davies, solicitor, Pontypridd, claiming compensation on behalf of the family of the late Rev. W. Landeg Powell, Caerphilly, as the latter had met his death when returning home from his Sunday engagement at the above chapel.

Our readers will remember that the Rev. W. L. Powell was officiating at Pisgah (C.M.) Chapel on the Sunday previous to the collision. He was paid the usual fee on Sunday evening, and left for Clydach Vale, where he stayed till Monday morning.

It is a very unique case, and whether they can rightfully claim or not remains to be seen.

Probably no such case has happened since the Compensation Act has become law, and the case will undoubtedly attract

Taff Vale Disaster.

Compensation Claims at Pontypridd.

Judge's Important Decision.

At Pontypridd County Court on Friday before his Honour Judge Bryn Roberts three compensation cases arising out of the Taff Vale Railway disaster which occurred in January last at Hopkinstown came up for hearing. The first case taken was that of George v. South Wales Miners Federation, and which, it was stated governed the other two.

Mr. A. T. James (instructed by Messrs Morgan, Bruce, and Nicholas) appeared for the applicants, and Mr. Llewelyn Williams, M.P. (instructed by Mr. G. F Forsdike, Cardiff), represented the respondents.

Above and below: From *Rhondda Leader,* 11 October 1911.

Mr. James further stated that he was under a considerable difficulty, inasmuch as the wording of the section of the Act stipulated that they were not entitled to recover both damages and compensation. The proceedings were originally commenced with the view and in the hope that possibly the insurance company would be induced to compromise, having regard to the unfortunate circumstances. The applicants in these cases had, in fact, recovered damages against the Taff Vale Railway, and had been paid.

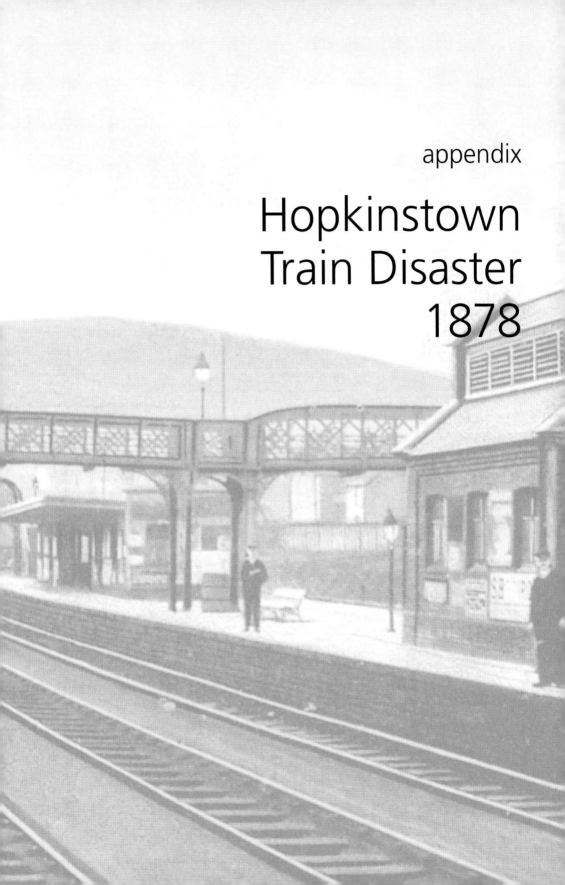

appendix

Hopkinstown
Train Disaster
1878

The Disaster of 1878

The tragedy of 1911 shocked the people of the area and it was hoped that recommendations made at that time would ensure that another disaster of this nature would never occur again. However, research has shown that a similar disaster did occur thirty-three years prior to this, in October 1878, within a half-a-mile of the 1911 disaster, with one of the trains involved coming from the Rhondda. Thirteen passengers were killed, either outright or from their injuries later, and many others were injured, both seriously and superficially.

With reference to the official Ministry Report issued by the Board of Trade, here is the story behind this tragedy:

Pontypridd Station is situated on the main line of the Taff Vale Railway between Cardiff and Merthyr and Aberdare. The Rhondda branch line from Treherbert joins the Main Line at the north end of Pontypridd Station, with the passenger traffic to and from this branch worked from a dock lying on the western side of the up main platform.

About a quarter-of-a-mile to the north of this station, a short double line called the north curve was constructed for connecting in an easterly and westerly direction this Rhondda branch with the main line, with double junctions formed at the two extremities of this curve. The Rhondda branch was called the Rhondda cutting junction, whilst the junction with the Main Line was called the north curve junction. This short connecting line was opened for mineral and goods traffic in October 1872, and appropriate signal boxes were erected at the two junctions, with points and signals interlocking, and co-ordinating to deal with up and down traffic.

The curve constructed was of a very short radius (about 7 chains, approximately 165 yards) and driven mostly through a rock cutting, and in consequence of the sharp radius of this curve, the view of the engine driver is limited in each direction and at no time would it have exceeded seventy yards.

In September 1875, the railway company commenced to work a new system for the empty carriages used for passenger traffic between Cowbridge, Llantrissant and Pontypridd, both of which served as terminal stations. Up to four passenger trains had been run daily in each direction between these places, and on the arrival of the trains at Pontypridd the passengers had disembarked and the train had drawn ahead, until the last carriage had cleared the points at the north curve junction with the up main line, and then waited for a signal from the signalbox for permission to push back (along the wrong road) the train of empty carriages on the up line from the

Rhondda cutting junction, and hence on to the down line of the Rhondda branch and back into the main station.

Very stringent safety regulations were in force at that time to ensure the highest levels of safety standards available when carrying out these shunting operations. Through experience, certain amendments were issued from time to time in order to maintain such standards by the company's traffic superintendent.

In general the regulations were as follows:

Taff Vale Railway
Cardiff 22 September 1875
Until further instructions the following must be strictly observed with reference to working the Llantrissant trains of empty carriages at Pontypridd station:

As soon as the passengers have all alighted, the guard will, with the carriages, proceed on the Main Line to the North Curve Junction, and will from that junction, on receiving a signal from the policeman, shunt the train on to the North Curve up line so far as the Rhondda Cutting Junction, when, on receiving a signal from the policeman at that junction, the train will proceed on to the down Main Line of the Rhondda branch, the train will then draw down. The engine is to take water and wait at its accustomed place before proceeding on to the down Main Line platform.

The passenger train brakesman of the Llantrissant train will, in every instance, proceed to the Rhondda Cutting Junction to inform the signalman that the train of passenger carriages has passed up to the North Curve.

So as soon as the down Rhondda branch passenger train has passed clear of the Rhondda Cutting Junction towards Pontypridd, an all-right signal of 'line clear' may be sent to, and must be acknowledged by, the signalman at the North Curve Junction; then the Llantrissant train of carriages may be shunted on to the North Curve up line.

While the Llantrissant train is standing upon the up Main Line, and until the train and engine have passed clear of the main line onto the North Curve, the up main line home and distant signals of the North Curve Junction must be kept set at danger.

The home and down signals of the Rhondda cutting junction must be kept at 'danger' after the passing of the down Rhondda branch passenger train until the Llantrissant train of carriages has passed out and proceeded on towards the Rhondda junction with the main line, leaving the North Curve Junction perfectly clear.

Every precaution for the safety of these and every other engine and train must be strictly observed.
James Hurman, Traffic Superintendent

However a further amendment to these regulations was issued on 30 September 1875.

Commencing tomorrow, Friday, and until further instructions, the guard of the Llantrissant passenger train will, after the arrival of his train at Pontypridd Station, remain there in charge of parcels and letters brought by that train, and deliver same to the different trains for destination. The brakesman will, in the guard's place, proceed with the train of passenger carriages to the North Curve, and U.D. Rees, platform porter, is instructed to proceed to the Rhondda Cutting Junction instead of the passenger train brakesman to inform the policeman at that place that the train of passenger carriages has proceeded on to the North Curve, as per instructions issued September 22.

J. Hurman

Although these stringent safety regulations were in force from 1875, and were conscientiously applied up to the time of the accident in 1878, it would appear that outside circumstances and human error attributed to this disaster. Further investigation deemed that negligence on the part of William Roberts, signalman in the employ of the Taff Vale Railway was the contributary cause of this disaster. (See page 83.)

In order to appreciate the circumstances leading to this disaster it is necessary to be familiar with the timings of the trains involved in the collision from their respective stations and the times of arrival at Pontypridd Station.

The Rhondda train would have left Treherbert at 3.35 p.m. and would reach Pontypridd Station at 4.21 p.m.

The Cowbridge (Llantrissant) train would leave at 2.15 p.m. and would reach Pontypridd Station at 4.13 p.m. This train arrived at Pontypridd Station at this time, and, after discharging its passengers, proceeded up the line to the North Curve Junction, where it waited until the Rhondda train had been signalled as having passed down to the station over the Rhondda line, and passed the Rhondda Cutting Junction. Upon receiving such a signal the Cowbridge train would then proceed to the Rhondda line, and then back to the station for its return journey to Cowbridge behind the Rhondda train as far as the Treforest junction, then proceeding towards Llantrissant.

As mentioned earlier, this curve was limited in its view in each direction and resulted in there being an obstruction between the two signalboxes placed at each end of the junctions.

From the regulations imposed, it would be the duty of the signalman at the Rhondda cutting junction to signal the other signalman situated in the box on the north curve junction that the Rhondda train had passed and was proceeding towards the station.

This procedure having been carried out, the Cowbridge train would then be shunted, tail foremost, through the deep cutting of the Rhondda line, and then to follow the Rhondda train (at a safe distance) into the station. However, as fate would have it, this was not to be on this Saturday afternoon of 19 October 1878.

The Disaster

The 2.15 p.m. passenger train from Cowbridge, which consisted of engine and tender and five carriages, arrived on time at Pontypridd Station, and after its passengers had disembarked, the train then proceeded to make its way to the north curve junction, where after waiting for the required signals it arrived at 4.15 p.m.

As the train pulled in to this junction, the signalman, Mr William Roberts, came out of his signalbox and signalled to the driver of the train, John Morgan, who disembarked from his engine and walked back to the steps leading to the signalbox, where Mr Roberts handed him a package.

The signalman then continued up the steps to his signalbox, called out 'all right', and the brakesman (and guard) Peter Griffiths, who was at the brake carriage at the rear of the train which had stopped almost opposite the signalbox, then gave the 'all right' signal to the engine driver to set back, and the train then proceeded at around 4/5mph back to the Rhondda cutting junction.

Later, when questioned, William Roberts stated that as he went up the steps leading to the signalbox, he thought he heard two rings of the bell from the Rhondda cutting signalbox, and the he gave the signal by calling out 'all right' to the brakesman for the train to proceed. However on entering the signal box he saw that the needle of the telegraphic instrument was standing at 'Junction Blocked', and then realised that he had made a mistake, but had no means by which he could stop the train at that moment.

The 3.35 p.m. passenger train from Treherbert to Pontypridd consisted of an engine and tender, brakevan, six third-class carriages, one brake carriage, one first class, one second class, two third-class carriages, and one brake van, arranged in this order. The train was due to arrive at Pontypridd Station at 4.16 p.m.

The train was running on time, at a speed of approximately 11mph, and as it passed over the Rhondda cutting junction points, the fireman, Mr Shadrach Okay, who was standing on the left side of the engine, called to the engine driver, David Thomas, who was on the right side of the engine, 'Look out, Davy, the Cowbridge train is into us'.

He didn't see the Cowbridge train before the collision took place.

Mr Peter Griffiths, the brakesman riding in the brake carriage, was about fifty-five yards from the Rhondda passenger train when he saw it coming towards him. He immediately applied the brake with one hand and signalled the driver and fireman of his own train with his other hand, but the signal was given too late. The collision occurred at that time, the train speed at the moment of collision being estimated at 2/3mph.

The result of this collision was catastrophic, with the empty Cowbridge train striking the brake van, which was situated next to the tender of the engine of the Rhondda train, grazing the following two third-class carriages, and badly smashing the third and fourth third-class carriages, which resulted in three carriages of the passenger train being completely thrown off the rails, together with the brake van and carriage of the empty Cowbridge train. This devastation resulted in the deaths of many of the passengers, together with many serious and minor injuries to others.

People came quickly on the scene to render what aid they could to the injured and to help those who had escaped injury from the wreckage. People then did what they could, in turn, to help others still trapped. The local doctors, Leckie, Rhys Hopkins, Dixon and Mc.Loughlin, hurried there to render assistance and to give advice to the helpers. Other doctors outside of the area, on hearing of the disaster, also made haste to the area; these included Dr Henry Naunton Davies, Porth; D.W. Davies and N.W. Davies, Llantrisant; Ivor Lewis, Cymmer; Idris Davies, Ystrad; Rhys, Treherbert; and Vashell, Porth. These valuable hands ensured more assistance to the injured.

By this time a large crowd of onlookers had gathered, with many offering help where possible. The local police, who were quickly on the scene under the supervision of Superintendent Mathews, Inspector Thorney and Sergeants Rees and Jones, were able – due to the crowd present at the disaster being so orderly – to assist in the rescue operations.

By this time many of the dead and injured were lying beside the track of the wrecked trains. Arrangements had been made to transfer many of the injured to the hospital wards of the local workhouse, which was nearby, for further treatment. The wards and the infirmary were quickly filled, and others were then transferred to the local Union hospital. These arrangements were ably carried out by the local police force.

A large workshop near the collision area was quickly converted into a temporary morgue where the bodies of the unfortunate victims were laid prior to later being transferred to the facilities at the Union Hospital, where they could be identified by relatives or friends.

Due to the confusion created by the number of dead and injured, a true picture of those who died and those who received injuries was not available until 25 October 1878.

A copy of the details of the dead and injured is shown:

COLLISION AT PONTYPRIDD.
October 19th, 1878.

Deaths.

Davies, Evan Owen, aged 38, of Dowlais
Thomas, David, „ 50, of Porth
Jones, John, „ 24, of Trealaw
Clarke, Thos. Phillip, „ 35, of Cardiff
Thomas, Sarah, „ 70,
James, Phœbe, „ 61, of Aberdare
Davies, David, „ 53, of Aberdare
Lloyd, David, „ of Porth
Davies, John, „ 24, of Hafod
Parry, Jeremiah, „ 47, of Heolfach
Parry, Mary Ann, „ 45, of Heolfach
Ratigan, Patrick, „ 67, of Pontypridd at Cardiff Infirmary.

} at Pontypridd.

Injuries.

Name.	Occupation.	Residence.	Nature of Injury.
Williams, J.	Saddler	Chapel St., Pontypridd.	Bruise of shoulder.
Lewis, Wm.	Not stated	Pwllewn, Graigwen.	Contusion of right leg and chest.
Richards, James	Draper	Treforest	Injury, left knee.
Lewis, Thomas	Not stated	Graigwen	Bruised head and left shoulder.
Watkins, William	Labourer	Pontshonorron.	Contusion and bruise, left thigh.
Morgan, Thomas	Moulder	Tramroad Side, Treforest.	Contusion of face, slight injury to head, and loss of teeth.
O'Donnell, Mrs.		High Street, Pontypridd	Contusion head, face, and body.
Rosser, Barbara, Miss.		Llwynpia	Leg broken, both bones.
Walters, David	Labourer	Penygraig	Compound fracture, both legs.
Beard, Wm.		Treorky	Severely bruised about head.
Morgan, John		Treforest	Severe contusions and bruises.
Harris, Mary		Heolfach-Ystrad.	Compound fracture, right leg, and dislocation of wrist.
Williams, Thomas		Llantrissant	Fractured ribs.
Jones, Wm.		Llwynpia	Both legs fractured.
Married woman		Penydarren	Both legs hurt.
Phillips, Lewis		Pentre Ystrad	Hand bruised.
James, John		Do.	Much unnerved.
Rowlands, Evan			Severely scratched.
Thomas, George	In Ironworks.	Beaufort	Contusions, each leg.
Thomas, Wm., son of above.		Do.	Scratches, each leg.
Not known	Publican	Vaynor	Severely. Not expected to live.
Jones, son of Mrs.	Bookseller	High Street, Merthyr.	Roof of mouth knocked in
Powell, Moses	Collier	Tynewydd	Bruised leg and severe, shaking.
Morgan, Miss Alice.		Ystrad	Bruised legs, and shock.
Jones, Miss J.		Glanynant	Contusion, right calf, and shock.
Frazer, Mr.			Bruises and shaken.
Phillips, Margt. Ann.		Mountain Ash	Bruised arm and leg, and shaken.
Jones, Jno. L.	Painter	Ystrad, 162, High St., Merthyr.	Left leg and face bruised.
Marshall, Frank	Working for Mr. Davies.	Treherbert	Slightly injured.
Jones		Hopkin's Town.	Injured arms, shoulders, and legs.
Crockett		Tonyrefail	Rupture and bruise of leg.
Morgan, Wm., jun.		Danygrove	Sprain and contusion, calf and leg.
Williams, son of Mr.		Canton	Said to be severely injured.
Gardner, son of Mr.		Do.	Shock.
Quick, Ridney		Treforest	Abrasion of cheek, contusions, and swelled ankles.
Walters, David	Collier	Llwynpia	Both legs broken.
Thomas, David	Not stated	Ton, Ystrad	Arms, back, and left leg injured.
Thomas, Gwenllian. Wife of do.		Do.	Wound right side of head, and left leg injured.
John, Rees	Collier	Do.	Badly shaken, and complains of leg.
Dorington, Chas.	Mason	Pontypridd	Teeth and head injured.
Williams, Henry	Painter	Coed Penmaen.	Leg and arms, fracture of thigh.
Thomas, Elizabeth		Ystrad	Head.
Beard, John	Quarryman	Pontypridd	Head cut, body bruised, and contusions.
James, Iago	Not stated	Treherbert	Lacerated wound, with contusions right leg, and other injuries.
Higgs, George	Do.	Pontypridd	Both thighs badly bruised.
Parker, George	Do.	Do.	Abrasion of left fore-arm near elbow, and contusions.
Williams, Evan	Do.	Ystrad	Both legs broken.
Cross, Tom or Wm.	Labourer	Treforest	Right leg broken.
Evans, John	Platelayer	Porth	Fracture of both thighs.
Twain, S.	Telegraph lineman.	Cardiff	Fracture of ribs, lower jaw left thigh and leg.
Manning, John	Labourer	Stormstown, Pontypridd.	Injury to back and legs.
Griffiths, Sarah		Swansea	Fracture of left leg near ankle joint.
Karslick, George	Builder	Penygraig	Amputation of right leg.
Jones, Edwin	Collier	Heolfach	Fracture of both legs.
Morris, Wm.	Do.	Dowlais	Fractured patella and wounds.
Cook, Chas. or Jas.	Miner	Burton, Somerset.	Contusions left eye.
Parry, Wm. James	Collier	Ystrad	Concussions and contusions.
Morgan, John	Not stated	Tony Pandy	Amputation of left leg.
Davies, David	Boilermaker.	Aberdare	Fracture of left thigh.
Jones, William	Not stated	Heolfach	Sprain of right instep and contusions.
James, William	Mason	Aberdare	Severe scalp wound and slight concussions.
Evans, William	Collier	Trealaw	Fracture of right leg.
Jones, William	Timberman	Tony Pandy	Fractured thighs, right leg, wound of right thigh, wound in left popliteal.
Jones, Thomas	Tailor and draper.	Dowlais	Dislocation of hip.
Mies, Henry	Moulder	Mountain Ash	Compound fracture of left leg, wound of lower lip, abrasion of right leg and cheek.
Phillips, Catherine		Gilfach Goch	Right and left legs bruised.
Harris, Thomas	Collier	Ystrad	Left leg broken.
Harris, Edward	Do.	Heolfach	Fractured leg and rib.
Richards, Morgan		Coed Penmaen.	Contusion and lacerated wound and bruises and right leg.
Jones, John		Coedraw	Contusion of right ankle joint.
George, David		Duffryn Terrace, Ferndale.	Forehead cut; right foot badly injured.
George, John		Do.	Swelling on foot.
Nicholas, David		Do.	Two legs slightly bruised.
Evans, John		Underhill House, Ferndale.	Legs bruised, and back of head much swelled.

Name.	Occupation.	Residence.	Nature of Injury.
Polgrain, James	Engine driver.	Pontygwaith	Bruised chest.
Davies, Willm.	Collier	12, Union St., Ferndale.	Leg injured.
Evans, Sarah Jane.	- - -	Llwynpin	Left side of head and face, and shock nervous system.
Jones, John	- - -	Cwm Clydach.	Bruised face, hand, hip, and spits blood.
Lewis, David	- - -	Do.	Lacerated wound on head.
Rogers, F. H.	- - -	Tony Pandy	Leg and head and nervous shock.
Jones, Mary Ann	- - -	Llwynpin	Shock. No external marks.
Badham, Wm.	- - -	4, Edward St., Canton.	Wound right temple and general shock.
Morris, Wm.	- - -	- - -	Injured head.
Cross, George.			
Boy, unknown.			
James, David	Sinker	Havod	Cut on leg and neck.
Williams, Danl.	Collier	Cymmer	Slightly injured.
Griffiths, Mrs.	- - -	Porth	Fractured leg, slight wound on head.
Morgan, Wm.	Carpenter	Tonyrefil	Slightly injured.
Evans, Mary Ann	- - -	Llwynpin	Shock.
Morgan	- - -	Ton Ystrad	Bruised.
Wife of Do.	- - -	Do.	Do.
Thomas. *qu.* Roberts, John	Collier	Dowlais.	
Pugh, Owen	- - -	53, High St., Tredegar.	Walking lame. Apparent injury to knee.
Morgan, Sarah	- - -	Brook St., Ystrad, now at 22, Cross St., Penydarren.	Contusion right arm and shoulder, and right side, and left hip and leg. Had two fits at Merthyr. Subject to fits.
Phillips, David	Collier	Pentre	Contusion right hand, and bruise on right ankle.
Name unknown	- - -	Tonyrefil	Slightly injured.
Do.	- - -	Ferndale	Do.
Do. (female)	- - -	Do.	Do.
Williams, Thos.	Collier, Llwynpin.	2, Union St., Tredegar.	Contusion right knee and calf of leg.
Williams, Jenkin	- - -	Cowbridge	Reported himself to station agent as injured, but denied by Dr. Stanistreet.
Granger, Mrs.	- - -	Cymmer	Leg and arm bruised, cut over eye.
Granger (son of Do.)	- - -	Do.	Left leg injured.

This is a list made up to to-day's date, Friday, October 25th, 1878.   J. HURMAN.

The Enquiry

During Saturday evening and Sunday, numerous officials of the Taff Vale Railway, including Mr J. Hurman, traffic manager and Mr Perry, chairman of the company, together with members of the board, Messrs. C.H. Williams, W.D. Bushell, and colonels Gould and Saville, visited the scene of the disaster, not only to make enquiries into the cause of the catastrophe, but to express their deepest sympathy for the sufferers, and to ensure that no expense was spared in providing whatever might be necessary for the surviving victims.

All through the weekend many people visited the workhouse hospital enquiring about the health of their relatives and loved ones.

Meanwhile the two signalmen, Stephen Ellis and William Roberts, were suspended pending an inquiry into the cause of the disaster. However, due to the verbal statement given (at that time) by William Roberts it was assumed that he was responsible for this tragedy, and on that Sunday evening Superintendent Mathews called at his cottage to take him into custody on a charge of manslaughter. Despite this charge, he was allowed to remain in his cottage, together with his family and with a constable present, until the hearing the next day at the Magistrates Court.

That day he appeared at the court to answer a charge of manslaughter, with Mr W.H. Morgan acting for the prosecution, and Mr Stephens, Cardiff, acting for the defence. After formal evidence had been given by several witnesses, the prisoner was cautioned as to any answer he might make as to the question of his guilt, to which he stated that he reserved his defence.

The stipendiary magistrate addressed the prisoner to inform him that he would be committed for trial on a charge of manslaughter in a higher court, and this would take place at the next assizes in February 1879.

The prisoner was allowed bail, which was tendered by Revd E. Roberts, Tabernacle, and Mr J. Roberts.

The Trial(s) at the Assizes

On Thursday 13 February 1879, at the Glamorganshire Assizes appearing before Mr J.B. Maule QC, Mr William Roberts surrendered to his bail to answer an indictment charging him with manslaughter of Mr Jeremiah Parry on 19 October 1878.

Mr Henry Allan (with Mr David Lewis) appeared for the prosecution, and the prisoner was defended by Mr Bowen Rowlands (with Mr Arthur Lewis). After the initial opening of the proceedings outlining the circumstances of the case for the prosecution the following witnesses were called and examined by the prosecuting council and the defence council. They were: Police Sergeant Evans, John Morgan, engine driver, Morgan Aubrey, fireman, Peter Griffiths, brakesman and underguard, Samuel Roberts, engine driver of the Rhondda train, Stephen Ellis, signalman, James Hurman, traffic superintendent of the Taff Vale Railway, Jabez Mathews, superintendent of police at Pontypridd, and Dr Rhys Hopkins.

It would appear from the evidence given that although Mr Roberts' behaviour was the main cause of the accident, other factors outside of his control and which had been carried out by others also contributed to the accident whilst the anomalies in the system of working procedure proved it to be quite inefficient and had been condemned by the Board of Trade! (See page 89/90.)

His lordship, having summed up in great depth, invited the jury to retire to consider their findings and to reach a verdict. The jury was then absent for roughly an hour-and-a-half, before returning to the court. The foreman of the jury then stated that there was no prospect of them agreeing upon a verdict.

The learned commissioner then discharged them, and the prisoner, Mr Roberts, was admitted to bail, to appear again for trial at the next general assizes at Swansea in August of that year.

At the Glamorgan Assizes at the Guildhall Swansea, with Mr Justice Manisty in attendance at the Criminal Court, Mr William Roberts, aged fifty-four, a signalman, was once again indicted for killing and slaying Mr Jeremiah Parry on 19 October 1878.

The following were sworn in on the grand jury:
Messrs H.H. Vivian, MP (foreman), J.C. Fowler, Howel Gwyn, Griffith Llewellyn, G.B. Strick, Arthur Gilbertson, G.B. Brook, S.S.H. Horman-Fisher, the Mayor of Swansea, T.A. Marten, C. Bath, J. Jones, J. Jenkins, Clarke Richardson, W. Graham Vivian, James Lewis, Rhys Hopkin Rhys, R.A. Essery, John Crowe Richardson, John Poddon, J. Aubrey Vivian and H.N. Miers.

The prosecution was conducted by Mr H.G. Allen and Mr David Lewis, whilst Mr Bowen Rowlands and Mr Arthur Lewis were council for the prisoner. Mr James Hurman, traffic superintendent of the Taff Vale Railway, stated that the prisoner had been a signalman in the employ of the company for twenty-six years and was considered a man of exemplary character. On the day of the accident the prisoner handed the witness (Mr Hurman) a statement in which he admitted that after speaking to the driver of the train (Mr John Morgan) which arrived at 4.15 p.m. and had come to a standstill, he ascended the steps of his signalbox, and on the way thought he heard the bell ring twice. This would have been a signal from Mr Ellis that all was clear, and the defendant said to the driver, 'all right Jack', meaning that he could proceed through the cutting. The driver then proceeded.

When the prisoner looked at the instrument in the signalbox he found that he had made a mistake, and that he ought not to allow the train to pass through. Mr Hurman stated that a different system of working had been adopted since the accident had occurred. Colonel W. Volland, who had carried out the report on behalf of the Railway Department, Board of Trade, had highlighted the defects in the signalling system.

The next witness, Mr John Morgan, the driver of the Cowbridge train, stated that upon receiving the signal from the prisoner he started the train and proceeded towards the Rhondda line. When he arrived between six and eight yards of it he saw the Rhondda train coming down. The witness was driving at 3 to 4mph, and although he reversed his engine he could not prevent an accident.

Under cross examining it became very clear that simply saying 'all right' should not be a proper signal for the witness to start. According to regulations a flag should have been used. When he got near to Ellis's signalbox he did not sound a shrill whistle as the regulations required, because he assumed that the line was clear. When he got to Ellis's box he did not receive a signal authorizing him to proceed onto the main line. He knew that a rule had been laid down to the effect that the driver should stop until he received a proper signal from Ellis to proceed onto the main line.

His lordship said that the point seemed to rest here – the driver went on without receiving any authority from Ellis.

Mr Allen remarked that the prisoner was stationed at his box to prevent the possibility of a train getting into a dangerous position, and it was owing to his mistake that the train got to a dangerous place in the first instance.

His Lordship remarked that the accident would not have occurred if there had been no disobedience of rules on the part of the driver.

Mr Allan: But would it have happened if the prisoner had properly attended to his duty?

His Lordship: But was the prisoner the actual cause of the accident?

Mr Allen replied that if the prisoner's negligence contributed to the accident he was amenable, although other persons might also be guilty.

His Lordship stated that it was for the jury to say whether the negligence was not too remote for them to be able to conclude that the prisoner was the cause of the accident. His Lordship then pointed to the jury the disobedience of rules on the part of the engine driver, and remarked that he appeared to have gone at a speed which prevented his stopping on seeing another train. It was for the jury to say whether the prisoner or the driver was the cause of the accident.

The jury then consulted, and the foreman stated that they were of the opinion that there was not sufficient evidence of substantial neglect which would justify them in attributing the accident to the prisoner.

The prisoner was then aquitted.

The Final Outcome

As it was stated at the trial of the signalman, Mr William Roberts, that the working practice in operation at that time had been condemned by the Board of Trade report issued by Colonel W. Volland, highlights of his findings should be considered. The collision had resulted from an improper and dangerous manner of working the Cowbridge train of passenger carriages at Pontypridd station, a method of practice employed since the year 1875.

The passage of the empty passenger train should have been properly controlled by out-of-door signals, worked from each junction signalbox, for the guidance of the engine driver.

He considered that the collision resulted from an error in the working of the absolute block system, by a mistake of a signalman in the working of traffic on a wrong line of railway, not provided with out-of-door signals to check any mistake which a signalman might make.

He therefore recommended to the director and officers of the Taff Vale Railway Company, that this system of working along the curve should be abandoned without any delay. Modifications to the line system should be implemented to prevent any trains being drawn or backed out onto the passenger lines without the consent of the signalmen at the two junctions; and as the curve is short and sharp it should be guarded throughout its length by check rails to prevent any vehicle from getting off the rails which might afterwards run foul of the passenger line.

Action: It would appear from correspondence that the majority of the items criticised in the report were implemented either immediately or within a very short time afterwards, certainly the system of signalling was carried out within a few days of the accident.

Modifications to the rail network, whilst acknowledged, were carried out when convenient, and as the railway network continued to develop with the laying of extra lines to cope with the demand of the rail traffic within the area, safety rules were amended as necessary.

The north curve was finally closed in August 1968 as being redundant to local needs, and the development of a more modern rail network.

Compensation

Sparse information regarding compensation to the families of the deceased or those badly injured is available. Obviously this was granted, but the only record of it occurring is that in March 1879, Mr John Morgan, who had lost a leg, claimed compensation of £1,025.00 (a fortune in those days), a cork leg, and a promise of employment when able to commence work.

The Taff Vale Railway Company obviously admitted liability (after the evidence presented by the court and the Board of Trade report) and one can only assume that others must have benefited from this situation.

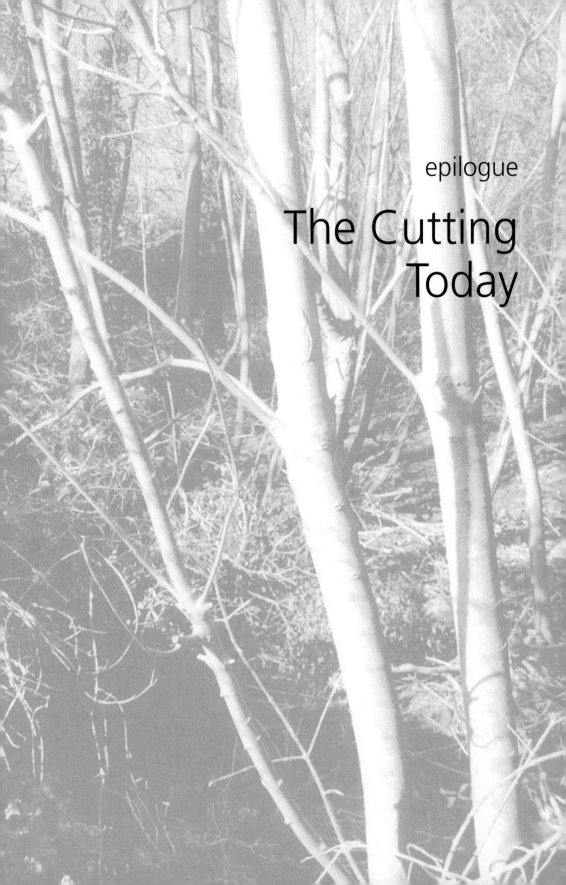

epilogue

The Cutting
Today

The Cutting Today

Due to various developments taking place in the area, little remains of the cutting. Approximately twenty-five yards from its entrance and its connection to the main railway line there lie the only remains of it today.

This section is overgrown and can hardly be distinguished, as can be seen in the accompanying photographs.

Above and opposite above: The front part of the cutting. Note the main railway line in the background.

Opposite below: The trees and undergrowth which have taken over the remains of the cutting.

Opposite above: More trees and undergrowth in the cutting.

Opposite below and below: The end section of all that remains of the cutting.

Related titles published by Tempus

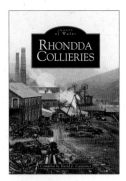

Rhondda Collieries
DAVID J. CARPENTER

This lovingly compiled volume records the valley's mining heritage, from the daily working of the mines to the sudden tragedy of pit disasters, and David Carpenter brings things right up to date, showing the uses to which the collieries are put today.

0 7524 1730 4

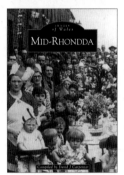

Mid-Rhondda: From Penygraig to Lwynypia
DAVID J. CARPENTER

Once a sparsely populated area, the Rhondda valley was industrialised with the arrival of coal mining. Around 180 images chart the rise and fall of the industrial society of Tonypandy, Penygraig, Trealaw, Clydach Vale and Llwynypia

0 7524 1156 X

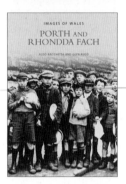

Porth and Rhondda Fach
ALDO BACHETTA AND GLYN RUDD

This, the third photographic collection on the Rhondda in this series by Aldo Bacchetta and Glyn Rudd, assembles a splendid mix of images and concentrates on Porth, the gateway to the Rhondda, and the Rhondda Fach, from Ynyshir to Maerdy.

0 7524 3011 4

Rhondda Revisited
EMRYS JENKINS AND ROY GREEN

This absorbing third collection of old images offers a nostalgic glimpse into the history of the Rhondda Valley during the last century, and features many aspects of everyday life, from schools and churches, public houses and shops, to transport, matinees and derbies.

0 7524 3388 1

If you are interested in purchasing other books published by Tempus, or in case you have difficulty finding any Tempus books in your local bookshop, you can also place orders directly through our website

www.tempus-publishing.com